Recollections on a Road Between

Recollections on a Road Between

A Story of My Life

EDWARD J. DUPUY

WITH A FOREWORD BY
JAY TOLSON

RESOURCE *Publications* · Eugene, Oregon

RECOLLECTIONS ON A ROAD BETWEEN
A Story of My Life

Copyright © 2024 Edward J. Dupuy. All rights reserved. Except for brief quotations in critical publications or reviews, no part of this book may be reproduced in any manner without prior written permission from the publisher. Write: Permissions, Wipf and Stock Publishers, 199 W. 8th Ave., Suite 3, Eugene, OR 97401.

Resource Publications
An Imprint of Wipf and Stock Publishers
199 W. 8th Ave., Suite 3
Eugene, OR 97401

www.wipfandstock.com

PAPERBACK ISBN: 978-1-7252-7228-6
HARDCOVER ISBN: 978-1-7252-7229-3
EBOOK ISBN: 978-1-7252-7230-9

Biblical quotations are from the NAB, USCCB, online: https://bible.usccb.org/bible.

To Jan, Ben, Shannon, Rylan, Madeleine, James, John, Lindsey, and Eli

Foreword

EDDIE DUPUY UNDERSTANDS THAT telling your own life story might be hardest story to get right. Who can see one's own life fairly—in the round, warts and all, at times triumphant, at others defeated, often inglorious, though occasionally glorious—without succumbing to the temptations to smooth it out with a definitive meaning or to arrange it along a simplifying arc? Resisting those and other temptations, Dupuy offers something far more truthful and valuable: a precise evocation of the restless unease and puzzlement with which a searching soul inhabits a lifetime—in Dupuy's case, a lifetime extending from the warmth of a Louisiana Catholic childhood through years of struggle with training to enter the priesthood to the decision to forsake that route for a different kind of journey, this one through marriage and the making of his own family, through teaching and literature, through never-ending thinking about and thanking for the given hardships and rewards of that curious passage across one's mortal span.

Jay Tolson, Editor
The Hedgehog Review

Society must assume that it is stable, but the artist must know, and he must let us know, that there is nothing stable under heaven.
 —James Baldwin, "The Creative Process"

Jesus thrown everything off balance.
 —Flannery O'Connor, "A Good Man is Hard to Find"

Acknowledgments

THIS BOOK BEGAN WHILE Jan and I lived in Abu Dhabi, UAE. I had thought of compiling a collection of my writings, interspersed with narrative context, and I began doing so in the spring of 2019. As I progressed, Jan said, "Why don't you write an autobiography?" I mulled it over a few days and then got to work. Readers can thank her for the suggestion, and you can fault me for deficits in execution.

Jan and my long life together remains a mystery, not only that we can speak of things that happened forty years ago, but that we sometimes agree about them!

Add to that the wonder of child-bearing, the arcs of our children's lives from infancy to adulthood, their marriages, and now their turn as parents—both perpetuating and correcting our wrongs. We have much for which to be grateful, despite many difficult times.

I thank, then, Jan and the kids, their spouses, and their children, without whom I could not have written this book.

I thank my parents, now several years deceased. They not only gave me life, but they pushed upon me, though I sometimes pushed back, the importance of education.

And I thank my brothers and sisters, who helped form me in ways known and unknown.

More practically, I want to thank Lindsey Bineau, our son John's spouse, who read and edited an early version of my autobiography and offered suggestions for developing it into what you now read.

Robert Green, Charley Matt, Sean Duggan, OSB, Jim LaVilla-Havelin, Beth Schumann, and Jan read early drafts of this work and offered guiding comments. For their time and interest, I thank them.

Acknowledgments

I thank my editors: Michelle Buckman, copy editor, who found more mistakes than I care to admit in what I thought a "clean" draft, and Matt Wimer, of Wipf & Stock, who patiently responded to my myriad questions.

I thank Allen Roy for encouraging me to enter the seminary, and I thank Larry Bronkiewicz for helping me discern my exit from it.

Finally, I wish to thank the Monks of Saint Joseph Abbey, the Jesuits at the Gregorian University in Rome, my confreres at the North American College, and my fellow students and graduate professors at Louisiana State University, particularly Lewis P. Simpson, James Olney, John R. May, and Fred C. Hobson. Though he wasn't at LSU, I also wish to thank John F. Desmond, with whom I corresponded many years and developed an old-fashioned epistolary friendship. Four of these five scholars are deceased, but their words and works still challenge me. They collectively opened spaces that I continue to explore today.

Introduction

How exceedingly great is the force of memory!...It is like a vast and boundless subterranean shrine. Who has ever reached the bottom of it?

—St. Augustine of Hippo, *Confessions*

What is memory? What is *memory?* Memory is what you remember. No you change the story, you "remember." A story, not a fact. Where are the facts? There is the memory, there is the truth—you don't know, *never*

—Daniel Mendelsohn, *The Lost*

If it is true that a pattern of one's life emerges in its telling, then the truth of a life and clues to its meaning depend not just on verifiable facts, but on memory and how memory evolves into narrative—a "re-membering" or a "re-collecting" of passing time into the passages of story.

First, then, I offer a few facts to set a broad context of my story. You might think of these facts as an outline of my obituary.

Born at Baptist Hospital in New Orleans on October 17, 1958, the sixth of seven children of Harvey Jerome Dupuy and Dorothy Miremont Dupuy, Edward Dupuy lived in New Orleans from birth to 1962, in Lafayette from 1962 to 1972, and moved back to New Orleans in 1972, where he graduated from O. Perry Walker Senior High in 1976.

He attended Louisiana State University, thinking he might become a mechanical engineer. After his first year at LSU, he left engineering to attend a seminary college, feeling called to the Roman Catholic priesthood.

Recollections on a Road Between

He finished a baccalaureate in 1980 at St. Joseph Seminary College, operated by the monks of Saint Joseph Abbey, which stands just outside of Covington, Louisiana. There, he became alive to the liberal arts. A year of theological studies at Notre Dame Seminary in New Orleans was followed by a year and a half at the Gregorian University in Rome, where he lived at the North American College. He left theological studies (and the pursuit of priestly life) in February of 1983. He was always deeply grateful for those years and their part in his formation.

From Rome, he returned to New Orleans where he worked as a Psychiatric Technician at Coliseum Medical Center and at DHL as an office manager in an office of one (himself). He was engaged to be married in 1984, a relationship that fell apart not long after the engagement. In April of 1985, he met Jan Fluitt, introduced to him by a high school friend and roommate at LSU, René deLaup. After a delightfully torrid summer, he followed Jan back to Rome (much to the chagrin of their parents) where she had a Fulbright grant to teach Italian English teachers methods of teaching English. They stayed there for about eight months before returning to New Orleans. In January of 1987, they married (much to the delight of their parents).

In May of 1993, he completed a PhD in English at LSU. He published a revised version of his dissertation—a study of Walker Percy and literary autobiography—in 1996. He also published several scholarly articles and reviews, and he wrote poetry. He held various jobs in higher education that took him and the family to Covington, Louisiana, back to New Orleans, then to Billings, Montana, Savannah, Georgia, and San Antonio, Texas. He retired from higher education in 2018 to follow Jan to her long-term post in Abu Dhabi, where they lived for four years.

Jan and Edward have three children, Benjamin (b. 1989), Madeleine (b. 1990), and John (b. 1992). They are married to Shannon, James, and Lindsey, respectively. Ben and Shannon have a child, Rylan (b. 2020), as do John and Lindsey, Eli (b. 2024). All of their children and their spouses live along the Puget Sound in Washington State, and Jan and Edward moved to Tacoma in 2023 to be near them.

Having presented the bare facts, I begin a story.

Recollections on a Road Between

In 2018, not long after Jan and I moved to Abu Dhabi, the capital city of the United Arab Emirates, we watched stage nineteen of the Tour de France on television—the grueling mountain stage from Lourdes to Laruns. Since our move to Abu Dhabi we had taken to viewing French TV when we could. Jan had lived in France in the early 1980s and was eager to practice the language. I studied French on and off since the fourth grade, but I never spoke it well. Neither of us did very well understanding the French commentators, however. "I'm not picking up any of this, are you?" she asked, and I concurred, but we kept watching, neither of us knowing much about current world-class cyclists or cycling in general.

Every so often the telecast would switch from the close-up shots of the racers, taken by cameramen on motorcycles or in cars, to an overhead shot taken from a helicopter. With those aerial views, the beauty of the Pyrenees, the Valentin River along the route, and the French countryside would be revealed.

"Let's go there," I half-joked.

"It would be cooler," Jan replied, referring to the intense heat and humidity of summer at our new home.

It was an old game we played. A beautiful setting in a movie might prompt us to say, "What a beautiful place. Let's go there." Or watching the Pro-Am at Pebble Beach along the Pacific and the magnificent Monterrey Peninsula: "Let's go there!"

We have been lucky to live in beautiful and historic American cities—New Orleans, Savannah, San Antonio, not to mention three years in the gorgeous state of Montana. We both studied abroad for extended periods—she in France, I in Italy. In the late 1990s and early 2000s, while living in and around New Orleans, we made three trips to Europe, so we have been "there," to astoundingly beautiful parts of the world.

I walked two or three mornings a week along Abu Dhabi's famous Corniche, a meticulously manicured park that runs about six miles along the coast of the Arabian Gulf. I went out before the heat cranked up, though it could still be very hot and humid in the early mornings. During those walks I usually saw several groups of immigrant workers or the occasional tourist enjoying themselves on the beach and in the water. Were they, like me, remembering their homes and family, connected to them by the water that also kept them separate?

Recollections on a Road Between

In 2004, we moved from New Orleans to Billings, Montana, where I worked for three years at a small college. I remember attending a meeting at Big Sky Resort as the school's representative for its participation in a National Science Foundation grant. A family vacation to Big Sky in 2002 placed Montana high on our list of places to move should an opportunity arise. In this case, "Let's go there!" was no joke. The drive from Bozeman and down highway 191 through the Gallatin Valley is one of the most beautiful drives in Montana, second only to that from Livingston to the north gate of Yellowstone Park in Gardiner—through the famous Paradise Valley.

At the conference I had the chance to reflect publicly on the connections that bodies of water can foster. The Yellowstone River flows north out of the park to Livingston. The Absaroka and Gallatin Ranges border the valley majestically, the river running strong and clear, and the ranchlands dotting the river's banks and up to the mountain fronts make for, well, paradisiacal vistas. At Livingston, the Yellowstone turns northeast, flows past Billings into the plains of Eastern Montana, eventually running into the Missouri River just southeast of Buford, North Dakota. The Missouri then runs to St. Louis where it pours into the Mississippi, which flows down the spine of the country to New Orleans and the Gulf of Mexico. One could, theoretically, put a message in a bottle in the Yellowstone River in Gardiner and retrieve it on the river front in the New Orleans French Quarter. I made such a point to the group gathered for the meeting—even though I was a transplant from New Orleans, we weren't all that separated. We were connected by water.

Norman Maclean, perhaps Montana's most well-known writer, ends *A River Runs through It* with the line, "I am haunted by water."

Now, as I remember these walks along the shore of the Arabian Sea, I see again people playing or relaxing, and I swim in the ocean of memory:

I remember our house in Billings, which sits on the northwest side of town, on a rise toward Billings' most prominent geological feature, the Rimrocks, what locals call "the Rims." The Rims form the northern edge of the main part of the city, stretching several miles east to west. At their highest point, they rise about five hundred feet from downtown Billings and provide stunning views of the Yellowstone River valley. Our house sits only about fifty feet above the city, but on clear days from the picture window in our living room, we can look out above the rooflines to the Beartooth Mountains sixty miles to the southeast and to the Pryor Mountains about the same distance due south. Scientists say that eighty million years ago—if anyone can fathom such an expanse of time—the Rims were part of the shore of the Western Interior Seaway, which stretched from the present-day Gulf of Mexico to the Arctic. Where our house stands would have been several hundred feet below the surface of the water.

We left New Orleans about fourteen months before Hurricane Katrina ravaged the Mississippi and Louisiana coasts in late August of 2005, ultimately flooding New Orleans. Early in the New Year of 2006, we travelled there to visit family and friends. The house we had lived in was spared, but driving around the city—uptown near the Universities, mid-city between Carrollton and Napoleon Avenues, and to the lakefront area (all places where Jan and I had lived both before and after we met)—we saw the dark mark of water lines that stained the siding of houses, some more than eight feet above the ground. Mountains of trash stood in the neutral grounds of the broad boulevards near the lakefront. The friends we visited told harrowing stories, their eyes tired and resigned, memories still raw.

Water nourishes, but it also destroys—as Hurricane Katrina made apparent. Like memory, water can be shallow or deep, expansive or confined, it can flood or trickle, be muddy or clear, creator or destroyer. Memory and water exist between dualities.

Narcissus fell in love with himself while staring at his reflection in a stream, and Normal Maclean writes a memoir about his family, about the sacrament of fly fishing, about his brother's untimely death, and about the remembered river that connects them. Maclean follows an ancient tradition.

After telling the reader his story of conversion in the first nine books of *Confessions*, St. Augustine reflects on memory and time in books ten and eleven. He thus sets a template of autobiographers' attempt to combine the "what" and the "how" in writing their life.

With typical honesty, Augustine says that we think we know what time and memory are until we try to write about them. Augustine marvels (to God) about the "force of memory," how "exceedingly great" it is. He continues: "It is like a vast and boundless subterranean shrine. Who has ever reached the bottom of it?" One can easily imagine the ocean depths as Augustine's "boundless subterranean shrine." When he turns his brilliance to time, furthermore, he discovers a tri-partite "present": the present of time past, memory; the present of time present, awareness; and the present of time future, anticipation. The present, always between past and future, is not simply an instant; it can be broken into infinite instances. More a river than a series of instances, the present continually retreats into the past and races toward the future.

Augustine's genius, however, is his recognition that narrative might capture the present because it combines what James Olney calls "a single activity of dual dynamic: recalling a story backwards and telling it forward." Augustine probes memory, his boundless subterranean shrine, to recount his past (and thus write himself) confident that God will accept his confession in the present of writing and into the future. Memory nourishes his telling while it also becomes a subject of his telling.

Maclean's haunting waters recall the death of his brother, which he comes to terms with (in writing) through his book.

But memory isn't always so easily accessible. Samuel Beckett, to choose a modern exemplar, writes from a stance apart from God and with the seeming absence of memory. In *Krapp's Last Tape*, for example, the eponymous character makes tape after tape, caught in the infinite regress of memory, trying to connect to and tell his past in memory and trying to remember the trying to tell in memory. Beckett calls into question the ability of the past to establish a present self and thus the self's ability to write itself into existence. For Beckett, whatever self we might possess, forever cut off from the boundless shrine of memory, is also forever separated from itself, let alone from God or others.

Augustine taps memory's vastness and thus tells of his new life in God. Haunted by the waters of memory, Maclean finds words that might tell the story of his brother's death. Through Krapp, Beckett grapples with memory and is frustrated at its inability to bring him to solid ground.

What does all of this have to do with my story?

As a child of the modern world, I relate to Beckett. His continual attempt to gain a foothold speaks to me. For my story is one of beginning, time and again, not only in a large, sometimes unwieldy family, but in a variety of jobs and places, in a country founded on an idea that continually manifests itself somewhere between that idea and its lived reality. At the same time, Augustine and Maclean also speak to me. All three writers feed (or try to feed) on the fathomless depths of memory to nourish a self, to connect to a past that might not only "write" them into existence, but also speak to incessant and sometimes failed attempts to do so.

At the water's edge, in the shifting sands of the Arabian Desert, through the evanescent beauty of television images, I, too, am haunted, somewhere between time's ceaseless flow and the immeasurable power of memory, forever seeking a place.

Let's go there—on this road between.

～

Here's another story.

I have played golf since sometime in 1965, when I was seven years old. My father started playing in his early forties, and I took lessons from the club pros at Oakbourne Country Club in Lafayette, Louisiana, where my dad splurged for a family membership. While I didn't play at all while living in Italy, neither as a student nor later when I lived there with Jan, golf has been a constant in my life.

An absurd game, golf can be like life, a Sisyphean sport that uses as its prop a small ball instead of a boulder. You play rounds (endlessly beginning). Perfection is impossible. Even the best players call it a game of "misses." Utterly boring to many—Mark Twain famously called it "a good walk spoiled"—for me golf taps the drama of life

Playing partners (ostensibly competitors), are more like fellow wounded pilgrims trying to navigate the course, which along with yourself, stands as your real competitor. Despite this, I might say, with some schadenfreude, "Tough break," when I see my playing partner's golf ball nestled against a tree or eight inches underwater!

Golf is a head game. Like many sports, to play well requires a sense of self-mastery, overcoming ever-lurking demons. "You" launch the ball that is, in a sense, another "you." Depending on your current relationship with your dark specters, you may land in the woods, the rough, or the irenic fairway. A playing partner, seeing a ball in a sand trap, might ask, "Is that you?" Your disappointed response: "Yes, it's me." You play another shot, and another, and another, none ever the same as the ones before. The hole ends, the round ends, but you always start again with a clean slate—the next hole, the next round, like another day, another minute, another present moment.

Golf sometimes haunts my dreams.

For years, I've had a recurring dream in which I stand on a tee box getting ready for a shot. I have the driver in hand. As I bend over to tee the ball, the ground below me begins to undulate, and I realize I'm in a space too cramped to swing. As the ground moves, I struggle to get the ball onto the tee. When finally the ground stabilizes enough for the ball to stay in place, I begin my pre-shot routine—check my grip and alignment, get into a balanced stance (or try to). The ground begins to move again, and there's no room to swing. I wait—for the ground to quit moving, for my feet to stop sinking and rising, for space to open. It doesn't. And so I stand off-balance and cramped, frustrated and disappointed. I wake without having hit a shot.

I have not always known what to make of this dream. Sometimes I think of the old sports adage, that to excel one must stay "balanced, focused, centered," which would lead me to conclude I'm just a bad player. Other times, I see the dream as emblematic of my fear of action or performance. What if I hit a bad shot? Should I choose to not hit a shot at all, so as not to fail?

Every now and then, I think of Paul Tillich, the famed Lutheran theologian.

While in the seminary I read collections of his sermons, one volume of which is titled *The Shaking of the Foundations*. Tillich argues that such shaking can offer a way to see beyond stable positions fostered by family, culture, religion—or sports. He writes:

> Man is not God; and whenever he has claimed to be like God, he has been rebuked and brought to self-destruction and despair. When he has rested complacently on his cultural creativity or on his technical progress, on his political institutions or on his religious systems, he has been thrown into disintegration and chaos; all the foundations of his personal, natural, and cultural life have been shaken (*Shaking Foundations*, 6).

He goes on:

> There is something immovable, unchangeable, unshakeable, eternal, which becomes manifest in our passing and in the crumbling of our world. On the boundaries of the finite the infinite becomes possible (*Shaking Foundations*, 9).

Wait a minute! What? How did you get from golf to Tillich? The finite to the infinite? On boundaries?

Perhaps my unconscious mind knows more than my awake mind, and Tillich's shaking offers the best understanding of my dream—and a good part of my life!

Could it be that disruption and imbalance have fostered consistency in my life? Is it possible to come to a greater sense of self through periods of interruption and disruption—physical, emotional, intellectual, or spiritual?

Can "shaking the foundations" form a paradoxical bedrock of experience, a sort of foundationless foundation? Can it offer a path to things "large and unknown," as Annie Dillard once said, and perhaps, as Tillich suggests, "eternal?"

My life encompasses several moves, difficult loss, and upheavals in thinking, all accompanied by periods of depression and profound doubt, but it also includes an abiding sense that things will be OK.

As I read Tillich, and later Walker Percy, I saw myself in their works. In the preface to my book on Walker Percy and autobiography, I tell a short story of the effect Percy's writing produced in me:

> I gradually realized that this man was writing about me. It was not an altogether pleasant realization, for if you know Percy's characters, you know that they are a rather wounded lot. How could he know me so well? How could he show me my own wounds?

Since the time of my book's publication, I have met several readers of Percy who tell the same story. "He's writing about me," they invariably say. They speak of a sense having been startled but also awakened to a greater sense of themselves and their struggles.

In one of his essays, Percy writes that "the wounded [person] has a better view of the battle than those still shooting."

Woundedness, while unpleasant, opens a space. If one is wounded in battle—or in life—one exists both as a part of and apart from those presumably unwounded. I think Percy's comment suggests that woundedness and the awareness of it make a space for getting on in the world. It may be a deep, unstable, and shaky space, but it is space that opens possibilities for a fresh way of seeing. That space furthermore, is experienced as both nowhere (from where does this wound come?) and now, here (I sense my woundedness in the present).

In my story, in the ocean of memory, I hope to offer a fresh view of the "battle"—a struggle for myself and the shaky, between place I inhabit in the world.

Recollections on a Road Between

One of my poems, written in 2015, speaks to this shifting "betweenness":

Beggars at the Table

What is it that ties
a person to a life with
words and rhythm or
lines and color, a promise
of hope and love by
a seemingly silent God?

What accounts for the fervor?

Don't speak of muses
or daemons, spirits
or visions or will!
Don't talk of genes
or hemispheric
bifurcations or
functional scanning
or neural pathways!

These are chimera,
Plato's shadows on the wall—
domesticated expression,
a suburb of form and shape.

Speak rather of human hearts—
corrupt and pure, mendacious
and true—always conflicted,
tripping, falling, sputtering,
the inner city
rising to a beat unknown,
beggars at a feast
where the host invites
them to be seated

at shifting tables
on chairs with little bearing
for food that dissolves
when they reach to make
shape and form
love or hope, rhythm,
beauty or truth.

⌒

Here's yet another story.

In my first semester in grad school at LSU, fall 1987, I enrolled in a seminar called "Modern Poetry" led by James Olney, the same fellow who led seminars on literary autobiography. James more or less founded that field with his book *Metaphors of Self*—and he eventually became my dissertation director.

A brilliant man, he seemed to have read everything. This impression was reinforced when he invited me and some classmates to his home, and we gazed, somewhat awed, at his personal library—a very large book-lined room, meticulously ordered. He wore bow ties and suits to seminars, rarely raised his voice, and seemed the incarnation of the "gentleman-scholar." When I walked into Allen Hall, which housed the English Department, I often spied him behind his editor's desk in the office of the *Southern Review*. He appeared so focused that his entire world became the manuscript he held.

Learned, humble yet authoritative, and collected, he seemed the antithesis of me. In my first semester of graduate study, I developed an eye twitch, a case of hemorrhoids, and a persistent itching that, when scratched, created small whelp-like lines where my nails passed. I later learned it was called dermatographia—"writing on skin"—a condition brought on by stress. My skin wrote the story of my anxieties, a series of chaotic etchings, like the enigmatic marks in the caves of Lascaux or a painting by Jackson Pollack.

On the first day of the poetry seminar, Olney polled us on our familiarity with the topic. When my turn came, I said, "I'm not horribly familiar with modern poetry." He chuckled and later used "horribly" in a quick summary of the polling results. "A blunder," I thought, as I scratched my neck.

Recollections on a Road Between

We read T.S. Eliot in the class. By that time, I had been reading Eliot for a few years, having come across him in my seminary studies, drawn to his gargantuan intellect and his religious sensibility. As a student in Rome, I bought a copy of his *The Complete Poems and Plays: 1909-1950*, from the American Bookshop near the Keats-Shelley house in Piazza di Spagna. I discussed "The Wasteland" with fellow seminarians, one of whom had a copy of Ezra Pound's mark-up of the early draft, and read and reread Eliot's final version. "The Journey of the Magi" and "Four Quartets" were also favorites. At St. Joseph Seminary College, I had played the character of the Third Tempter/Knight in a production of "Murder in the Cathedral," so I reread that and read his other plays for the first time.

When it came time to choose a topic for a paper in Olney's seminar, then, Eliot seemed the right choice for me. I was especially interested in his turn from what seemed like a modernist despair and loss in "The Wasteland" to a non-modern hope and unity in "Four Quartets." I read Peter Ackroyd's *T.S. Eliot: A Life*, and came across Pound's taunting couplet about Eliot's conversion:

> Let us lament the psychosis
> of all those who abandon the Muses for Moses.

I worked hard on the paper, one of the first in my new studies at LSU. My eye twitched relentlessly. I longed for a Rosetta stone to decipher the marks on my skin. Though I hadn't read everything there was about Eliot's conversion, I had read enough to know that I was going against the grain of most Eliot scholars who saw a lessening of Eliot's poetic prowess after his move to Christianity.

In the paper I set up the argument that the conversion, contrary to Pound's pithy summation, did not close Eliot's poetry into "psychosis" or monistic meaning, but actually opened it, meaning expanding widely from it. In my opinion, Eliot had not abandoned the Muses; his turn to Moses had opened his work to new possibilities.

I wasn't sure how James Olney would take it. Would he find it "horribly" naïve? When he returned the papers, his endnote said something to the effect of: "While your argument goes against most scholarship on Eliot, you have argued your case well." *Ah, relief.*

I don't have a copy of that paper because I culled many of my files in our move from Savannah to San Antonio many years later. I remember it now not only because of the stress I encountered in producing it, but also because of its emphasis on finding an opening despite apparent closure. In his later works, Eliot found a passage, if you will—through Pound's influence (for which he was often grateful)— into an expansiveness of time, memory, and history.

In the benefit of retrospect, that paper set a stage for the work you read now. I seek possibility and awareness of an opening by recalling the past and telling it now, making space for a self, perhaps space for you—perhaps, even, space for a golf swing.

Later in my time as a grad student at LSU, when I took my first class on Literary Autobiography with James Olney, I recall his asking about Richard Wright's *Black Boy*: "How did Wright overcome his background of poverty, racism, and negligence? Why was he not stifled, like so many others, by his 'history'?"

I can't formulate, even now, a good answer to that question, but I think it might have something to do with Wright's exploring his wounds and finding an opening, a passage, through writing.

I did not suffer the brutal oppression and poverty that Wright faced. Nevertheless, like him, I seek passages flowing through (and from) time and memory. I set my shoulder to the stone, knowing the task never ends, always begins again—in the next sentence, the next paragraph, the next chapter.

In the shaking of foundations and in the re-membering and re-collecting of story, something new and open emerges, perhaps ill-defined and between, yet present here and now.

1

Autobiography is often something considerably less than literature…and always something rather more than literature…. It refuses…to be a literary genre like any other.

–James Olney, "Autobiography and the Cultural Moment."

When I was a student in Rome, I thought I could see "home" better. And from Abu Dhabi years later, I also sensed home in the "subterranean shrine" of memory: the peculiar loamy and rancid smell of the river as I walked along the levee, an odor of beer and urine and coffee in the French Quarter, places or food that evoked memories of parents, brothers and sisters, or our kids when they were young—Café du Monde, the Farmers' Market, the lakefront (with Jan!), red beans and rice, a shrimp po-boy or muffaletta, or bourbon on the rocks.

When I'm in New Orleans or when I speak of it to others, "home" becomes present.

But being at home doesn't come easily.

What is "being at home?" What is it like? Does it imply ownership? Can I be "at home" despite disruptions and displacement, that is to say, by not feeling at home?

⁓

I was born in New Orleans, and my earliest memories formed there. They are the vaguest of memories, some propped up by the gravity of grainy family movies, but residing still in the "I" who now writes.

One film shows the celebration of my baptism, with Father Ed Templeton (my namesake) chatting proudly with my parents. Another shows my first birthday in our house on Michael Street. The family gathers round a plump baby sitting in his high chair, a small cake with a single candle placed in front of him. As the family sings, the baby, attracted to this bright object, sticks his right index finger into its wick and extinguishes the flame. A short look of astonishment, his face reddens, and he screams silently, the celebration shaken by pain and fear. The family moves quickly to salve him. The camera shuts off, and when filming resumes the baby is giggling, icing lathered on his fingers and around his mouth.

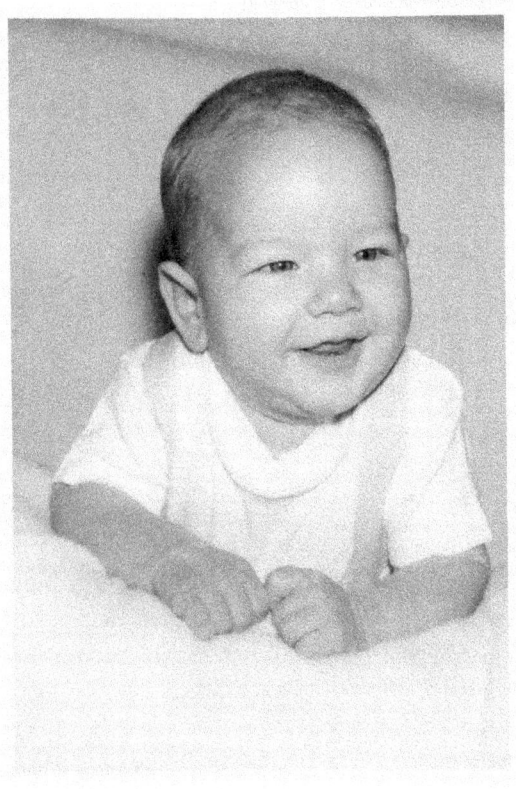

One of my baby pictures. New Orleans, LA, mid-1959.

Later, probably around two years old and now in a house on Cupid Street, I remember (or did I dream it?) rolling down the stairs. I tucked myself into the shape of a ball and tumbled down them repeatedly—unhurt—protected,

Recollections on a Road Between

I guess, by an ample store of lingering baby fat. I remember the stunt as a way of gaining attention in a household of six children, which in two years' time would be seven. I remember a Jetson-like tricycle that I rode around the neighborhood. I rode to a friend's house where I got my hands on some darts. An errant throw lodged one in the shoulder of an adult overseer. Was it a joke played on a very gullible young child, or did I throw the dart with force enough to stick in the man's arm? I don't know, but the image floats in the river of my memory.

My mother was one of five children, and my father one of seven. I knew my grandmothers but not my grandfathers. My mother's father, an alcoholic, abandoned the family when she was young. In her later years she described him as that "son of a bitch." Her mother moved the young family often because she could not always come up with rent payments.

My paternal grandfather committed suicide when my dad was young. My dad rarely spoke of his father, but if asked directly about him, he'd say, "We think he killed himself." My grandfather was the bookkeeper at a plantation outside of Baton Rouge. "Apparently," my father said, "he jumped into the Mississippi River after 'discrepancies' arose in the books." As I say, he rarely spoke of his father. Even when my brother-in-law offered my dad the chance to see his father's grave, after a long search and drive to it, my dad refused to get out of the car.

My parents met at a church softball league in Plaquemine, Louisiana. My dad was the first to go to college in his family, taking a degree in Education at LSU before World War II. He entered the Navy and asked my mom to marry him while stationed at Terminal Island, San Pedro, California. She travelled from Louisiana by train to San Pedro accompanied by her sister, whose job, assigned by my maternal grandmother, was to assure they married! They married on January 27, 1945, the same day, I learned years later, as the liberation of Auschwitz. My father was twenty five and my mother nineteen.

My dad shipped out for duty in the Pacific a few days after the wedding. He served as the skipper of LSM 452, which among other things, he successfully steered through Typhoon Louise. His ship formed part of the fleet deployed for the occupation of Japan, carrying Marines to Nagasaki after the city had been decimated by an atom bomb. I found out much later—online, of course—that LSM 452 was commissioned on February 1,

1945 (four days after my parents' wedding day), decommissioned on May 24, 1946, and sold on September 19, 1947 to Tacoma Boat Building Company. Tacoma! The place I now call home.

After the war, my father returned to LSU and earned another degree in the relatively new field of petroleum engineering. My mother worked various jobs, went to a two-year business school, but never earned a formal degree. She recognized the importance of education, however, and she made sure that all of us did well in school.

They were a beautiful couple. My dad—dark, heavy-bearded, handsome, and square—had a keen mathematical mind and a fondness for football, martinis, socializing, and golf. My mother—very pretty, not a delicate southern belle, but a hustler and a prankster with street smarts—was a stern disciplinarian. She could melt you into obedience with her eyes. She also enjoyed people's company, entertained often, and she was a good cook. At parties, she often observed more than conversed. Though their lives were marked by significant upheavals—the Great Depression, World War II, Auschwitz, Hiroshima, and Nagasaki—they rose, along with millions of others, in the post-war widening of the middle class. Their first child, Jerrie, arrived in December of 1946, and the last, John, in February of 1962, with five in between: Polly, Harvey, Jr., Debbie, Mike, and me.

My parents on their wedding day. San Pedro, CA, January 27, 1945.

Recollections on a Road Between

In their early days, my dad and the new family lived in Barataria, Louisiana, near the mouth of the Mississippi. Standard Oil of California (later Chevron) had a camp for employees there. They moved around south Louisiana—Baton Rouge, Lafayette, New Orleans. The move to New Orleans in 1972 was their last, and my parents stayed there, though not in the same house. In 1992, they moved to the fourth floor of a small condominium complex on the famed river in Algiers Point, a settlement across from the historic French Quarter. They lived there until their deaths in 2016 and 2017.

⁓

The first three children (Jerrie, Polly, and Harvey, Jr.) were born in rapid succession. "Three under three," my mother said.

Jerrie was a keeper of scrapbooks, follower of Micky Mantle and other sports heroes, social, and talkative. My mother said, "You can always have a real conversation with Jerrie." Thoughtful, and like many first-borns, possessing a strong sense of responsibility. She earned a degree in medical technology and moved to Houston in the mid-1960s, where she fell into a circle of friends (including priests and seminarians) with whom she still keeps in touch. She married Don Earthman, the Earthmans part of the patriarchy of old Houston, moneyed Catholics, socially connected, and generous with their wealth. Now a grandmother many times over, she is gracious not only with money, but with her time and her family. She and Don would have celebrated their fiftieth wedding anniversary in the summer of 2024, but he died suddenly and unexpectedly in May of that year. It is impossible not to mourn for the family, for Don was a genuinely good person, a loving husband, father, and grandfather.

Polly, less sure of herself than Jerrie, tentative, sometimes a flighty dreamer, cautious, more of the classic Southern Belle, pretty, homecoming queen in college, determined to work, earning an RN, engaged to a Louisianan who believed the state's motto—Sportsman's Paradise—went duck hunting and fishing with him, though she wasn't a sportsperson like him, called off the engagement, followed Jerrie to Houston, met a brash, confident Englishman (through Jerrie), married him, moved to Canada, and had my parents' first grandchildren. Polly died by her own hand in 1994 after falling into depression resulting from a prolonged bout with breast cancer.

Harvey, Jr., athlete (track, baseball, basketball, golf), followed our dad into petroleum engineering, but unlike him, left big oil for a series of independents, lived for a while in the Netherlands, where he met a German girlfriend. Harvey disappointed my mother when he was in college by "reading" *Playboy*. ("If you think it's okay to read this," she said publicly to the family, "let's put it on the coffee table.") He later married a Texas straight-talker and moved to Katy, Texas. Now retired, he watches documentaries, NFL football, and premier league soccer, plays golf, and enjoys family, home, and grandchildren.

Two years after Harvey, Jr., Debbie was born—brown complexion, fun-loving, energetic, hard-working. I once heard my mother tell her in high school, "If you want to date, then you need to stop hiding behind books." I don't know why my mom told her that; she was pretty, spirited, and likeable. She earned a degree in Speech Therapy, married a high-school sweetheart, and supported him while he attended Tulane Law School. They had five children, and she's now the matriarch of a passel of grandchildren. Gardener, traveler, Catholic in Catholic southwest Louisiana, fun-loving and energetic, welcoming, and probably the most like our mother in character.

Another two years and Mike came along—wiry hair, buck teeth (fixed by shiny braces); we called him, unkindly as siblings will do, "Curls and Coils." Driven to succeed, smart, athletic (basketball team captain, golf) SGA president, sold books door to door during summers in the rural US and earned enough money to buy a new Mercury Capri and later an old MG. Curls and coils gave way to a very handsome college graduate and med student. He graduated from Tulane Med School, specialized in anesthesiology in Los Angeles, moved to Phoenix, married a Phoenix beauty (a nurse), had three very handsome children, went through a prolonged and very difficult divorce, married again, and settled into the upper reaches of Phoenix society, where he plays golf, travels abundantly, and enjoys his grandchildren.

Four years later I was born.

Another four years after my birth, John arrived. Blond hair, blue eyes, he suffered from childhood ear infections, his teeth slightly yellowed in later life by repeated doses of antibiotics, attended an experimental elementary school (to the chagrin of our mother), fell in love with tennis in high school, came out as gay early in college, which he attended on a tennis scholarship. Handsome, smart, athletic, he, too, attended med school, specialized in dermatology. He tested positive for HIV in the mid 1980s. In the late 80s, while interning in Houston, he came down with opportunistic tuberculosis, got over TB and moved to Hollywood Hills in Los Angeles where he practiced at Kaiser Permanente. He contracted cryptosporidiosis, and as AIDS worsened, returned to live his last days with my parents in New Orleans. He died in September 1994, less than three months after Polly.

～

These brief sketches do not pretend to capture the lives of my siblings. Neither do they encompass my relationships with them. It goes without saying, though I will say it nonetheless: I tell the story of my life, written myself, and formed by my re-membering and re-collecting, which are very likely different from those of my siblings. Each of us sees, feels, recalls, and tells as the individuals we are, our viewpoints impacted by our age and lives at the time.

The immediate Dupuy Family. Destin, FL, 1993. Back (l to r), Eddie, Mike, Dad, Harvey, John. Front (l to r) Debbie, Mom, Jerrie, Polly.

Handled wantonly, memory and story can pull a family apart. Families are fragile institutions, threatened on all sides—by myths of fame, success, wealth, sex, and even religion, that can create hardened (closed) narratives, all propagated endlessly and instantaneously by a media-saturated culture. I hope to tread judiciously.

⁓

Because we were seven kids, and because Mom and Dad insisted that we perform well in school and in life, we were competitive, especially the boys. Who was the better golfer, basketball player, the smartest, the best looking, the hardest worker, the highest earner?

Harvey and Mike used to play basketball out on the driveway of our house in Lafayette. One night, Mike came into the house with a swollen hand. He said the ball had bounced off the roof and hit his thumb. Much later, we found out the real story, at least I remember it as such. He confessed that he and Harvey, who was more competitive than all of us, had gotten into a fight while playing. Mike swung hard with his left hand at Harvey's back—and broke his thumb.

I remember a "spoon" in one of my early sets of golf clubs—a four-wood carved from persimmon and painted blue. I used to practice with it in the back yard. Once John was standing too close to me when I was about to swing. I told him to move. When he didn't; I swung anyway. The gash above his eye bled horribly. Ma'malle, my mother's mother, was at home babysitting, and I remember the profound disappointment on her face when she found out what I had done. "I asked him to move," I said lamely. She staunched the blood with a wash cloth, trying to soothe my crying brother, and I sulked guiltily away.

It is hard not to see the classic story of Cain and Abel repeated in these episodes—jealousy and competition leading not to fratricide but to a broken thumb and a bloodied head. Love and fraternity overcome by rivalry. The stain of being human!

When I was in grammar school in Lafayette, I admired Mike's drive and his status as team captain and SGA president. And his golf game. I joined my parents, Harvey, and Mike as a young fifth golfer. Harvey and Mom were patient with me on these Sunday outings after church. My father and Mike could be irritated by my beginner's play. I needed encouragement, and Harvey offered to give me a quarter if I drove the ball past a small hump on the eighteenth fairway.

The girls stayed home with John and prepared Sunday dinner. Debbie—always the most domestic, Polly—kind, soft spoken, and Jerrie—direct but thoughtful. Did they resent staying at home while we were out playing golf? When I was young, it never crossed my mind.

We were a family on the move. After Jerrie and Polly moved to Houston, I remember road trips to visit them. My dad became frustrated and confused in navigating the big city by car. On one trip, he said he "didn't like the way this street ran" and abruptly turned the wrong way on a one-way street in the busy medical district. When we finally found their place, he was happy to see his girls and their young friends and became as buoyant as he had been frustrated in getting there.

Years later, someone gave him for Father's Day or his birthday a placard of a grouchy-looking dog (a boxer, I think) that had a dialogue bubble above its head: "My mind's made up," it said, "Don't confuse me with the facts." Able to laugh at himself, he could be at the same time easily frustrated and short-tempered. He put the placard on the prominent bar in our house on Mimosa Court in New Orleans—a testament to his personality, perhaps also a reminder not to take himself too seriously.

When we moved back to New Orleans in 1972, Mike, John, and I were the only children at home, but Mike was away most of the time—in Lafayette at college during the school years and selling books in rural America during the summers. So, John and I were alone with Mom and Dad from about 1972 through 1976, when I graduated from high school, then went to LSU and later to St. Joseph Seminary College.

John and I formed a strong bond, which occasionally required that I, a scrawny high schooler, protect him. One day, at the bus stop, I saw one of his classmates standing over him in a threatening position. He pushed John, who dropped his bag of books. I ran from where I was waiting for my ride to school, and though I was not much larger than the bully, I shoved him to the ground. He got up, embarrassed, and said, "Why don't you pick on someone your own size?" My clever retort: "You are my size!"

This happened before I knew John was gay, so I wasn't protecting him because of that, though I would have. I just thought it was my duty to stand up for him, and my unusual aggression could have been a response to my having been bullied both at the small Catholic school I attended in Lafayette and in my first year at public school in New Orleans.

In Lafayette, a classmate used to seek me out on the playground and regularly rough me up. After a while he resorted to making me pass out, telling me to hold my breath while he squeezed me tightly, which resulted in short periods of unconsciousness. I preferred passing out to getting roughed up.

In 1972, during my first year of public school in New Orleans, a fellow used to harass me after I got off the bus, demanding that I give him my lunch. In Civics class, another fellow hit me each morning as he walked past my desk. The teacher, a young African American coach, my first black teacher, counseled me to assert myself, which I did, and the bullying stopped—for a while.

Although I was athletic, I was not a jock, a category that implies attitude more than athletic prowess. When I was awarded the physical education medal at the end of that first year in public school, a jock lamented publicly in class that he couldn't "understand how a fag like him (pointing at me) could be given the phys ed award." I had no idea I had stirred up such animosity or such misimpression of my identity.

In any case, perhaps my defense of John rose from the classic school of hard knocks I had experienced. Our closeness later may have risen from empathy for his difficulties hiding his identity, his eventual coming out, and his lingering sickness.

~

In 1962, four years after my birth and just after John was born, we moved from New Orleans to Lafayette. I remember nothing of the physical move, though I do have recollections of our first two houses there. One was a small yellow house that had a water pump shed behind it. The other a white clapboard house on Arlington Drive with an oak tree in the front yard.

Because I have no solid memories of it, the yellow house must have been very temporary, simply a short-time holding place.

The white house provided a greater sense of home. My parents became friends with some folks across the street. They had a bunch of children too, all roughly the same age as us. My first friendship was with one of them, who went with me to pick blackberries in an overgrown drainage canal. I enjoyed these unsupervised times, though I also kept a wary eye open for poison ivy, snakes, and relentless mosquitoes.

Each year, army caterpillars infested an oak tree in the front yard. And each year my father burned them off with gasoline. It was thrilling! The caterpillars, clearly evil, had to be destroyed. My father, clearly good, served as the destroyer. I'd like to say that somewhere in my growing consciousness I objected, but I didn't. If I thought about it at all, I thought of it as my father taking on his parental duty to protect the family. The smell of the gasoline, the flash of flames, the charred caterpillars and the seemingly unscathed tree made me dance crazily, like David before the Ark of the Covenant.

Much later, when I was married with children, I used to protect my kids from fire ants in the backyard by burning their mounds with gasoline. The kids found the flames fascinating, but burning the ants didn't work. While some on the surface burned up, the fire forced the remainder deeper into the ground, only to rise again a few days later in a place nearby.

Like the yellow house, the white house provided temporary lodging while we waited for the completion of a new house that was under construction. My parents had bought about three quarters of an acre in a new development. It was their first new home. A family movie shows my mom and dad inspecting the building site with pride, walking on the foundation, talking with contractors, and fulfilling what came to be known as the mid-century dream, but also providing more space for them and their large brood.

Even though the details of the move are lost to my memory, I must have been sad leaving the white house because it meant moving away from friends on the street.

Nevertheless, I sensed my parents' excitement about the new house, which also fostered a feeling of permanence. My mother's brother, Uncle Ed, came for visits with his large family. He shared my mother's playfulness, but while she often restrained herself, Uncle Ed liked to push boundaries—as though to pick at my mother for her control. For a while, he drove an Oldsmobile 442 (a muscle car) to our new place in Lafayette. When it was time to leave, he hit the gas and left rubber in the street. My mother shook her head and clucked her tongue, mostly for the kids to see. But I think she liked his antics because she shared his impish character.

The house was large enough to be a gathering place. Jerrie and Polly brought home friends from Houston, some of whom, as I said, were seminarians or priests. One fellow, large, hairy, and portly (a future bishop as it turned out), had a big laugh and enjoyed telling stories: "My housekeeper wonders why there's so much hair in the drain of my bathtub," he might say. "I tell her delicately that I'm a very hairy person and I can't help it falling off when I shower—haw, haw, haw."

Another fellow, thin with straight dirty-blond hair and wire-rimmed glasses, looked like a scholar. He played the piano and entertained us for hours with tongue-twisting ditties. Though they never cursed—my mother spelled out her cursing ("Oh d-a-m-n")—my parents enjoyed these mildly bawdy songs as much as I did:

> Sarah, Sarah, sitting in her shoe shine shop.
> Sarah, Sarah, sitting in her shoe shine shop.
> All day long she'd sit and shine
> All day long she'd shine and sit
> Sarah, Sarah, sitting in her shoe shine shop.

My mother, in the midst of what she later called, her "religious period," enjoyed having these young folks in her house as much as she enjoyed the sisters from the Marianite convent in New Orleans, one of whom was her first cousin and to whom she once loaned our station wagon for a road trip they had planned. She also befriended the "Grey Nuns," who had a convent not far from our new residence.

From my point of view, my mother was always "religious" and thus never out of phase. She bowed her head when she passed by a Catholic Church. She attended novenas, and she herded the large family each weekend to Mass, something expected; no complaints allowed.

Once, however, she complained, years later, when Larry, my spiritual director in Rome, the presider at Jan and my wedding, and eventual godfather to our children, came for a visit to our house in New Orleans. As though she had bottled it up for decades and could not express it except in anger, my mother argued passionately that the church's stance on birth control and contraception had placed an undue burden on her early years of marriage. She used Larry as her "pounding board," holding him responsible, it seemed, for the church's stance. Larry listened passively, as though he'd heard it before from others, but said nothing. Jan and I listened in astonishment. As though relieved to have finally said it, after this outburst, my mother spoke nothing more about the topic, at least not in my hearing.

I don't remember complaining about church as a child. If I had such thoughts, I kept my mouth shut.

Recollections on a Road Between

In a large family, I learned to negotiate anger by keeping quiet. I realized later, when Jan and I had our own children, my mother might indicate disapproval more by silence than an attempt at tactful dialogue. When something particularly angered her, however, she would let loose, like she did with Harvey and the *Playboy* magazine, or when John was bussed to that experimental school instead of being allowed to attend the one in our neighborhood. It was best to stay out of her way. Jan expresses anger more directly than I have ever been able to do, and she sometimes gets frustrated with my bottling things up.

In any case, the large, rambling house offered a sense of continuity for me, a semi-solid place in which I became more aware of myself and the world.

I remember Jerrie, Polly, or Debbie sitting outside in front of the large air conditioning unit, curlers piled in their hair, using the warm air blown by the compressor's cooling fan to dry their hair. They sometimes kept an eye on me in a backyard big and open enough to play football or softball, or for my older brothers to practice their golf short-game.

My father barbecued on a pit fashioned from pipe casing used for drilling oil wells. I could never lift the heavy lid, but my dad managed with one hand, and Harvey and Mike did it, with two hands and some strain, a sign of their muscle, and their competitive spirits.

I remember the coulee (a drainage canal) behind our house. Although tree-lined, the coulee nevertheless snagged errant softballs or footballs, which if not retrieved, were left to rot in the smelly water. Small trails at the base of steep banks hid honeysuckle, blackberries, poison ivy, wasps, mud daubers, opossums, armadillos, lizards, skinks, and snakes. A dying tree fell across the coulee just behind our backyard and gave easy access to the neighborhood across the street behind us. Before the tree fell, we often tried to jump across the water when it was low. A water pipe behind a house about three down from ours offered another short cut across the coulee, but I didn't have the balance to walk across it like my friends did. If I wanted to get to the other side, I walked along the street, the long way around, or shimmied across the pipe on my behind, still wary of losing my balance and falling into the muck.

My father was not a hunter and didn't own guns, but I remember longing to own a BB gun. Mike had a pump action pellet gun (cool!) and because I wanted to be like him, I needed one. For a birthday or Christmas one year, I got a small Daisy BB gun as a gift.

One day, I took an old model of an F-4 Phantom and shot at it out by the coulee. I didn't see her coming, but my mother walked up behind me and gave me a stern "think-of-the-kids-who-don't-have-toys" lecture. She made me feel awful about nearly anything she didn't approve, so I felt awful after her tongue lashing. Although I said nothing, I also I thought she made too much of it and harbored some anger about her chastising me.

Later, I thought I shot a blue jay with the Daisy, and I spent several days in heaviness and dread, not knowing whether I had hit it or not. From then on, I confined myself to shooting at plastic army men perched on the bench of our redwood picnic table. BBs lodged in the soft stained pine and eventually rusted.

When my mother wanted to get rid of stale bread, she'd say "Throw it to the birds." It mimicked a favorite and common phrase that indicated her displeasure or disgust: "That's for the birds." Mocking birds, jays, cardinals, and sparrows visited our yard like pigeons in Piazza San Marco. I devised a plan to catch one: I took a light wooden box, perched it at about a 45-degree angle on a sturdy twig to which I attached a long piece of twine. I placed a scrap of bread under the box, hid behind the day-lilies that surrounded the patio, and waited. I almost caught several birds, not thinking of what I might do if I actually snared one. Lucky for them (and me) I didn't.

I remember "moving the bricks." My mother lined her gardens with bricks. Before weed eaters, if you wanted to trim the grass next to the bricks, they had to be moved so the lawn mower could get to it. I hated the job. As a seven- or eight-year old, I had a hard time hoisting (and then putting back) the eighty or ninety bricks. Moving the bricks required stamina. They were heavy and sometimes stuck in mud from frequent spring or summer rain showers. I never knew what sort of creature I might find underneath them—a small snake, earth worms, a centipede, rolly pollies, ants, or the dreaded "pincher bugs," whose pincers sometimes grabbed me before I knew they were there. They lay in the moist, dark earth, surprised by the sudden light that pierced their home.

My hands got filthy from the mud and earth, and they smelled odd—a peculiar loamy odor, the odor of decay and death, of grass, leaves, insects returning to soil—earth (humus), and it was difficult to wash off fingers and from under nails, like Macbeth trying to remove the stain of blood, the stain of death.

Death intruded even as the garden and the grass around it grew. My father's mother died in a nursing home, as did my mother's mother. One of my father's nephews, a pilot in Vietnam, went missing in action and was declared dead. One of my mother's nephews, the oldest of Uncle Ed's children, Jimmy, was also killed in Vietnam—a box of munitions exploded as he unloaded it.

I remember Jimmy's funeral—a morose occasion where the usually ebullient and mischievous Uncle Ed looked lost in grief. His wife, Aunt Rose, a beautiful, fiery Puerto Rican, dissolved into loud weeping. I can't recall what feelings I had as I stared at the flag-draped coffin. I must have felt sadness and fear because of Uncle Ed and Aunt Rose, whose displays of grief shook what I had come to know of them.

I had no overt political sensibility, but I remember worried talk with my friends about whether the war would be ongoing when we were older—a fear of being asked to serve. Whatever politics I possessed was derived from my parents and my wish to please them.

I wonder now if my memories of balance and guns, my dread at the imagined death of the jay, my turn to shooting at plastic army men, the deaths of my grandmothers and cousins, and my eventual attempt at catching a bird instead of shooting one signaled an inchoate turning toward my current beliefs about life and war and nature.

Could the imbalance I felt trying to cross the pipe suggest a nascent shakiness with the culture that was forming me? Was my anger at my mother's chastisement for shooting up my toy an anger not only at her, but an unconscious anger about the war in Vietnam, the F-4 an iconic symbol of that war?

Was shooting plastic army figures only play? Was I shooting at the "bad guys" whose aggression caused my cousins' death? Was I shooting a symbol of war, and thus wishing it gone? Was I shooting at an image of my own unspoken anger?

I see now that my feelings were contradictory. The thought of killing a jay weighed heavily because I might have taken the life of a beautiful living creature, but I didn't feel that dread when I went hunting with Polly and her fiancé and used a small gauge shotgun to shoot a waterfowl he called a "coot." Were coots, like ducks, made for shooting, but not blue jays? I was happy to have hit my target and felt I had proved myself in her fiancé's eyes, who had earlier in the day complained to her of "babysitting" me while out in the marsh. Were the Viet Kong, like coots, made for killing, but not Americans?

In Lafayette in the mid-1960s, is it possible that my actions, my early encounters of death, confusing and contradictory, might have spoken of a growing sense of unease and shakiness at the country I called home? Although memory sometimes supplies connections that a conscious mind cannot, it is impossible to say.

One day, I came home from school to learn that my mother had fallen and broken her leg. She was carrying John, who was probably only two or three, and she slipped on wet concrete, fell and hit her shin on the edge of the driveway. The break required a plate and four screws to hold the bone in place. She had a noticeable scar and lump for the rest of her life. When the plate and screws were removed, my mom put them in a plastic bag as unique souvenirs, playfully showing them to visitors as she might the Murano glass she years later brought home from Italy. She was in a full leg cast for many weeks, but I recall her getting around in a wheel chair or crutches—even sewing at her Singer where she made dresses for my sisters and mended shorts or jeans for the boys.

Clearly my mother's broken leg could have been a major disruption in family life, but I don't recall it that way. Instead, we kept moving apace. Playful as well as stoic, my mother didn't (or wouldn't) allow a broken leg to slow her or the family down. The wheelchair became a director's chair. She asked the girls to fix meals and tend to the toddler, John; she asked Harvey to pick up Mike and Debbie from after-school activities. I don't recall her ever having allowed herself to wallow. Instead, she managed the scene as though it were a test of will, creating a tableau of ease, even a cause for humor, suppressing whatever personal weaknesses the broken leg might have brought to surface.

I write this now in light of her lingering sickness and eventual death.

My mother had a congenital heart valve leak that manifested itself only after her eighty-fifth birthday. She declined a complicated surgery and lived for another five years with the increased bloating and other deleterious effects of congestive heart failure. Sometimes her legs grew so swollen they wept. She knew she was dying, and despite a lingering stoicism and wish for control, she sometimes lashed out.

Eight months before her death, in November of 2015, my father marked his ninety-sixth birthday. His short-term memory had long ago departed, and conversations with him inevitably circled round and round. "Where are you now," he might ask? "What are you doing?" When supplied with the answers, he'd say "Oh!" but ask the same questions a few minutes later. I called him on his birthday, but I didn't send him a birthday present, thinking that such a gesture would not register in his depleted and circumscribed consciousness.

The day after his birthday, I had a call from my mother. She chided me in no uncertain terms, telling me I was thoughtless, intimating I had no concern for my father. Though I was then in my mid-fifties, I felt like the child who shot up the F-4, though without the residual anger.

I knew that my mother had lost so much control, that her will had, as it must, given way, and that the tongue lashing served as an attempt to revive it. The call left such an impression, however, that I sent my father (via Amazon) several boxes of his favorite caramel popcorn just after getting off the phone.

My mother later apologized, first through a phone call from my sister Jerrie, and later when I saw her in person. Near her end, my mother was skeletal, a far cry from the beauty, vigor, and mischief she possessed nearly her entire life.

After my mother died, my father could not remember her death. "Where's Mom?" he asked, as though expecting her to walk out of the kitchen into the living room. When we told him she had died, he looked down, paused, and asked, "What did she die of?" We told him she had a bad heart, which had finally given out. Again he paused, looked down. A few minutes later, he asked again, "Where's mom?"

I don't know if he relived the hurt of her death each time he asked about her. I do know that when I visited, it was hard for me to tell him the story of her demise time and again.

My father was not a complainer, and he rarely mentioned the aches and pains he experienced in later life, but one day, when I was visiting from San Antonio, he did complain. "I feel bad," he said. "I feel so bad, I think I'm gonna die!" The next day, he did.

I began school in Lafayette at a small Catholic school. I was a good, not a brilliant, student. I did what was required, got mostly A's and a few B's. A "C" would have been cause for a parental inquisition. I don't recall being attracted to any particular subject. I did well in all of them, though I was pushed by my parents to excel in science and math. While I sang in the choir, I enjoyed time spent out on the court, in the backyard, or the golf course much more. In short, I was following the lead of my siblings and my dad. Math, science, and sports.

Going to school. Lafayette, LA, September 1964. Harvey and Polly in the back, and (l to r) me, Mike, and Debbie in the front.

Beginning in fifth grade, I played basketball and peewee football in a small elementary-school league. In seventh and eighth grades, the competition broadened, and practice became more rigorous. I dreaded drills such as "corner tackling" in which a runner and tackler ran at one another in a right angle. The collision sent shocks through the nerves of my shoulder and neck—pains I still have today and attribute, only half-jokingly, to "an old football injury."

Recollections on a Road Between

In eighth grade, our football team played Lafayette Elementary, a public school. As we Catholics warmed up, we saw a hulk of a guy emerge in football pants from the driver's seat of the car he had just parked. *Hmm, we thought collectively (and smugly), how many years had this guy failed before eighth grade?*

I played safety and was the team's deep snapper. I was very small, probably five foot four and about 105 pounds, but since I was the only one who could deep snap with any precision (a skill I learned from Mike), I got the job. I was pummeled after each snap. Playing safety, I remember the "hulky" eighth-grade driver breaking out into the secondary where, of course, it became my job to stop him. I threw myself into his churning legs, got stuck between them, and felt like dough in an industrial mixer. He scored.

We were not a family of readers, so as a child I did not devour books. I remember, however, going to the library and picking out a book about a perpetual motion machine. I've forgotten the title, but I was captivated by the idea. It tapped into my young scientific imagination but also reminded me, I think, of my family, which was always in motion—basketball, football, golf, track, baseball, debate, dances, and church, not to mention school and the many projects that kept us busy.

I didn't begin serious reading until I attended St. Joseph Seminary College, and later graduate school. So, unlike many scholars and writers, I came to books and writing "late." My mother noted that she always felt she had to be doing something instead of reading—as though reading were not "doing something." My father read the newspaper religiously but rarely a book. Once, after helping Jan and me move our numerous boxes of books during one of our many moves, he said: "I regret ever having taught you to read." It was meant as a joke, but it held a truth. Busy-ness, not bookishness, fashioned my early years.

Busy-ness can be the antidote to self-reflection, the promoter of competition, the keeper of norms, the slayer of the always-lurking abyss and the awareness of woundedness. I became a busy model child, thinking science had all the answers, comfortable with the conventional narrative of "progress." I sought the "success" that would please my parents, set me on a par with my family, and, I thought, please me at the same time. For several years it did. Only later did I peek into the abyss (and longings) that books opened to me.

Recollections on a Road Between

The 1960s in the United States marked a tumultuous, turbulent, decade in our history. Civil rights, voting rights, the war in Vietnam, protests against the war, the counter-culture movement, assassinations, rock 'n' roll, drugs, and the rise of "free love"—issues we confront again as a nation—came to a boil then.

The Dupuy household remained steady and busy.

I think my parents sheltered me (sheltered the family) from the maelstrom of the decade because it threatened an overturning of the world they had come to know. I don't recall heated debates (or any debates) about civil rights around the dinner table because I think they did not occur. I do recall my father commenting that the Beatles' hair, when they appeared on the *Ed Sullivan Show*, was "too long," with the implication that hair length equated to morality. I remember repeating horrible racist jokes and generally absorbing the conscious and unconscious racism of the time—guiltless and with impunity.

Maybe some discussions took place, and I was just too young to comprehend, which could account for my not remembering. But I do remember watching the 1968 Olympics on television. I was almost ten years old. Two black runners from the US held up their black-gloved fists as the national anthem played during the medal ceremony. My mother told me they had disrespected the country.

Very few African-Americans attended my school, and those who did seemed happy, not angry or resentful. At the time, however, I would not have been aware enough to know.

I remember the front-page spreads about JFK's assassination in November of 1963, and television clips of the shooting. I remember watching the news about Jack Ruby shooting Lee Harvey Oswald in the basement of the Dallas courthouse. Both signaled something momentous, but at five years old, I had no inkling as to what.

Perhaps not so oddly, I don't recall the deaths of Medgar Evers or Malcolm X, though I do remember those of MLK and Bobby Kennedy. My guess is that Malcolm X would have been considered a radical, far beyond the safe world my parents offered me as a child. I don't know what my parents thought of Medgar Evers' death or whether it ever came up in conversation.

Recollections on a Road Between

I remember the deaths of Martin Luther King and Bobby Kennedy because I was older and because, I think, they were the right kind of activists, the kind my parents, even if they didn't agree with (in the case of MLK), could approve. King's nonviolent struggle and the religious underpinnings of his message might have resonated with them, and thus media coverage of his death stuck with me. The Kennedy family—Catholic, handsome, and tragic—could not but be mourned in our household, but there were the "right kind" of Kennedys too. My mother mourned Jack and Bobby, but could not stand Teddy, whose fondness for alcohol and extra-marital affairs may have reminded her too much of her father.

My mother played the soundtrack to *Camelot* endlessly on our big cabinet stereo, reveling in the romance of the Kennedy presidency propagated by the press. However, after Jackie Kennedy married Aristotle Onassis, she called her a "whore." I was surprised at such language coming from a woman who did not curse, but who rather spelled out curse words. "Oh, s-h-i-t," she might exclaim after making a mistake in cooking. During the hype surrounding *Jaws*, my mother read Peter Benchley's book and crossed out all the curse words as she read.

I digress only because my mother, though very kind, was not averse to using racial slurs when angry or when she went to one of her favorite stores, owned by a Semite: "I'm going to pick up something at 'The Jew's,'" and she would often speak of trying "to jew him down" on a price while there.

I wish I could say my sense of justice awakened early in my life, in the face of racist brutality, everyday racism, or protests against the war in Vietnam, but it didn't. I was too busy with sports or preoccupied with my growing self-consciousness and sexuality. If talk of justice arose, it came packaged as a lesson in the morality of "being nice."

Only years later, after the liberal arts captured my imagination, did a sense of justice awaken in me. I felt gut-punched, for example, the first time I read this passage from Walker Percy:

> People are always asking, Why don't you write about pleasant things and normal people? Why all the neurosis and violence? There are many nice things in the world. The reader is offended. But if one replies, "Yes, it's true; in fact there seem to be more nice people around now than ever before, but somehow as the world grows nicer it also grows more violent. The triumphant secular society of the Western world, the nicest of all worlds, killed more people in the first half of [the 20th] century than have been killed in all history. Travelers to Germany before the last war reported

that the Germans were the nicest people in Europe"—then the reader is even more offended. (*Message in Bottle* 105)

I was one of those "nice" people.

In graduate school, I read Richard Wright, Frederick Douglass, Zora Neale Hurston, Ralph Ellison, Langston Hughes, Alice Walker, and many others for the first time. Why weren't they part of my high school or college literature classes? It might have helped to run across, for example, these words from Douglass from his "Farewell to the British People": "The fact is, the whole system, the entire network of American society, is one great falsehood, from beginning to end."

Or this from his *Narrative* of 1845:

> What I have said respecting and against religion, I mean strictly to apply to the *slaveholding religion* of this land, and with no possible reference to Christianity proper; for, between the Christianity of this land, and the Christianity of Christ, I recognize the widest possible difference—so wide, that to receive the one as good, pure, and holy, is of necessity to reject the other as bad, corrupt, and wicked.

When I first read Ralph Ellison's description of mixing the tiniest bit of black "activator" into Optic White Liberty Paint, the hairs on the back of my neck rose. They rose again when his supervisor in the novel says:

> "Our white is so white you can paint a chunka coal and you'd have to crack it open with a sledge hammer to prove it wasn't white clear through!"

> "If It's Optic White, It's the Right White."

Black people lived in Lafayette in the 1960s, but not near us. They lived mostly on the far north or far south sides of town. We had a black maid, and I sometimes rode with my mother when she drove her back to her Northside home, happy that I didn't have to live in such a run-down neighborhood. Blacks served as caddies and maintenance workers at Oakborne Country Club. I felt unease (fear?) as we walked by the caddy/maintenance shack toward the pro shop. "Big Joe" worked at snack-shack at the turn between holes nine and ten. He had a big laugh to match his large size, asked how we were playing, and served us drinks and snacks. Was he happy? The thought did not occur to me then. Now, I wonder how he felt as he laughed and served us, a black man in a white man's world.

I think I saw "race" in Lafayette like that "chunka coal," so white I couldn't see any blackness underneath. It was there, but invisible.

I'd like to think that had I read Douglass or Ellison earlier, had there been discussions at school or at home, I might have awakened earlier to a greater sense of the "great falsehood." That belief may be hopeful thinking on my part. At that time, Douglass's "great falsehood" simply would not have been accepted.

I see now that history is not what our history books at the time taught. Love of one's country, like love of one's spouse, does not mean that criticism is unwarranted. Eliot writes, "History is now." The United States, along with other countries, seems to repeat its past. It again confronts (or denies) systemic racism and fear of "others." Some of its denizens, in the name of patriotism, stifle critical discussion of history, but the practice of thinking critically about race or oppression, thinking critically of history, "now," requires love and care, not censorship.

In the 1960s, life at home and in Lafayette were just not structured to foster criticism. What about now, here?

We know now, for example, that the Nazi regime in the 1930s looked to eugenic theories (and practices) in the United States to eradicate those whose lives the Reich deemed "unworthy of living." Likewise, Jim Crow laws in the American South provided models for laws to oppress and isolate Jews. Despite our history, here and now our nation seems bent, not on rectifying the past, but returning to it as an imagined golden era—golden, of course, not for all, but only for some.

⸺

For years in her condominium that overlooked Mississippi River, my mother kept prints on the walls of her bathroom: African-American children, shabbily dressed, standing in front of ramshackle cabins eating large slices of watermelon. When he visited my mother's condo, an African-American priest-friend told me he could not believe his eyes. I had no defense and agreed with my friend, though I didn't challenge my mother. She had told me a few times, perhaps to goad me, that she might in fact be "racist." She may have seen it as an inevitability of her background or she may have been turning, as the country turns as I write, back to a fallacious vision of the United States as a white, Christian country.

My parents were good people who sought a good education for their children and worked hard to give us a life better than the one they had grown up in. In that venture, they were successful. They were fun-loving and social, and provided well for a large family. Their goodness, however, like whatever good I might claim, was (and is) marked by the large and persistent stain of the South—and of our nation—growing larger with the literal and metaphorical blood of "others."

The United States struggles with the racism bred into its fabric—"All men are created equal," unless, it seems, you are something "other" than white and Christian. While matters have improved, human rights' failings in the United States persist and have sadly re-emerged like an insuppressible bad habit.

The United States commonly calls out countries for their abuses while ignoring our own—the homeless, decaying housing projects and tenements, poverty amidst plenty, squalor, low-wage, dead-end employment, expensive health care, poor public education. The US finds money to support all manner of guns and a massive military, but it often looks the other way when asked to help the poor and the downcast. Not only does it look the other way, it blames "them"—for "their" lack of initiative, for being "Welfare Queens," for having too many children, for "addictions," or lack of discipline. Remembering the displaced Native Americans and Africans in the service of lucre may be unpleasant, but remember we must, especially in a so-called "Christian" nation.

Marilynn Robinson, perhaps one of our sanest cultural critics, writes in her essay "The Awakening" from *The Givenness of Things*: "'Christian' now is seen less as identifying an ethic, and more as identifying a demographic.... History has shown us a thousand variations on the temptations that come with tribalism, the excitements that stir when certain lines are seen as important because they can be rather clearly drawn."

She goes on:

> Christian ethics go steadfastly against the grain of what we consider human nature. The first will be last; to him who asks give; turn the other cheek; judge not. Identity, on the other hand, appeals to a constellation of the worst human impulses. It is worse than ordinary tribalism because it assumes a more than virtuous

us on one side, and on the other, a them who are very doubtful indeed, who are, in fact, a threat to all we hold dear.

Millions of words have been written against injustice and for freedom. Countless lives have been spent in service to the idea that "all men are created equal" in this "one nation, under God." But a notion of individual liberty seems to have trumped a sense of collective well-being. Can a nation devoted to "individual freedom" persist as a communal body, particularly when hatred, neglect, and resurgent tribalism create ever more "clearly drawn" lines? The danger, as it was for Germany in the 1930s, consists in moving toward a nationalist collectivism, with murderous lines drawn against an-other or others.

Perhaps a road between and an appreciation of our inherent shakiness can offer some help to a beleaguered nation, a road that travels between a sense of individuality and community, and thus incorporates both.

And yet we seem torn apart. What sort of country is this? Like King Lear, I say "I am mainly ignorant of what place this is." Is it home? If so, no wonder I feel so shaky.

The USA is not the only country to struggle with the rights of its denizens. Nevertheless, its tendency to say one thing and do another, to forget its sins and lies while calling out the sins of others, creates an untenable myth that, instead of fostering "liberty and justice for all," harms memory and closes off spaces into arbitrary (and injurious) boundaries.

I speak of the current state of our union because the spoken and unspoken history of the USA, of course, forms part of my history, now, here. And while it has taken me some time (and a lot of reading) to shake my balance, open a space, and see the detrimental character of unfounded boundaries, I cannot now unsee them. With T.S. Eliot in *Gerontion*, I ask, "After such knowledge, what forgiveness?"

2

You found out more when you left where you lived.

–Flannery O'Connor, "The River"

In the late spring of 2019, my brother Mike and sister-in-law Shelley visited Jan and me in Abu Dhabi. They arrived with friends by cruise liner from Mumbai. We met them at the Abu Dhabi port amidst a welcome team of young Emiratis—some performing a traditional dance, fake guns and real camel sticks twirling, others passing out dates and luqaimats—the latter an Emirati delicacy much like the famous New Orleans beignet, although luqaimats are rounded into camel-dung-like orbs. As Jan likes to say, "There's nothing better than fried bread dough covered in sugar."

Shelley is retired and Mike semi-retired. Both had lucrative careers, so they have traveled a lot, especially in the last few years. They've been to the Galapagos, Australia and New Zealand, Bangkok and Vietnam, down the Rhine, up the Nile, to Scotland and Ireland and to any number of domestic destinations, including family outings to Pebble Beach to mark significant family achievements. A golfer like me, Mike enjoys rounds at some of the premier courses in the US, not only Pebble Beach, but Bandon Dunes, Pinehurst, and others.

During their stay, we talked about our childhood and the travels we made as kids. As two of seven children of parents born before the Great Depression, we marveled at the ease and extent of travel we enjoy today, much more than anything available to the middle-class of our youth.

Before she died, our mother would often say with pride, "This family sure gets around." My parents traveled together only after my dad retired. She coaxed my father into travelling around the world on the now defunct

TWA. They loved going to New York City to visit two of my mother's aged aunts, Jessie and Belle, who lived together for more than sixty years in Jackson Heights. In their early years, however, with private school tuition and seven mouths to feed, and later years (because of declining health) my parents confined themselves to short trips—and eventually to no trips at all.

And here we were in Abu Dhabi! Recalling the modest trips we took as a family, Mike and I agreed that we didn't feel deprived. Rather, we got from them much of what travel offers—a sense of a new place and a new self—or at least an experience of the relationship between place and oneself.

⁌

Travel, of course, takes one temporarily to a place that is "not home." Travel offers the chance to see "home" from a new vantage point, but it also opens a sense of new customs, new languages, and in some cases, such as the Middle East, new dress. Travel offers a sense of being between. *What is this I'm eating*, one might think? *Why do folks dress that way?* Or more importantly, *Why do they think as they do? How do these folks stick themselves into the world?* Travel opens a shaky sensibility, a heightened awareness that can break down some of the accustomed boundaries within which one usually lives.

⁌

Mike and I wondered how (and if) we ever managed to get all nine of us out together. In our younger years, the family cars were often huge Ford station wagons, the SUVs of the 1960s. They were cavernous, with bench seats front and back, no seatbelts, and a jump seat in the back (facing the rear).

I remember spending time in the jump seat, watching and sometimes waving to the cars behind us. On one trip I recall hearing a rough scrape on the roof, and looking out, saw our heavy grey-brown suitcase airborne, flying away from the car like a big, clumsy, rectangular Frisbee. It landed broadside on the pavement, and skidded to a stop. The knots our sailor-dad tied had come loose, and the jump-seat passengers had to sound the alarm about the flyaway suitcase. We used that suitcase on trips for a long time after. Whenever we pulled it out, I ran my hands over its scars as a reminder of its fantastical flight (and landing).

We didn't travel to exotic places and certainly not by air. A popular vacation was to Uncle Ed's house to visit him and our cousins in Baton Rouge, where we enjoyed less supervision and had plenty "toys" to occupy our time: go-carts, mini-bikes and a nickel slot machine. We sometimes travelled as a family, and we sometimes took the bus for a week-long stay during the long Louisiana summer. The house had an odor entirely different from ours, not musty and not clean, but a blend of the two. The water in Baton Rouge was so soft we had a hard time feeling like we had rinsed the soap off our skin.

It wasn't just the water and the smell; new freedoms and a type of exoticism opened to us. In Aunt Rose's Puerto-Rico-inspired kitchen, I experienced for the first time the slimy juiciness of mangos and the starchy heaviness of plantains. My aunt's younger brother, a Baton Rouge police officer who lived with Uncle Ed and Aunt Rose, came home in the evenings with stories that never would have been told at our home. Even the thought of these week-long stays in a different place during the hot and humid summers created a sense of longing for the delights we knew that awaited.

I suspect our cousins didn't enjoy their time with us in Lafayette, with its greater supervision, as much as we enjoyed our time with them in Baton Rouge. I remember well a time when the cousin nearest to me in age, Johnny, visited during the week of the Fourth of July. We celebrated with fireworks in the backyard.

Johnny seemed always to be getting into trouble in Baton Rouge, so my father probably kept a keen eye on him. I had left a fish bowl out on the patio because the turtle I kept in it had died and I was airing it out. Johnny saw the bowl and promptly dropped a lighted firecracker into it. Of course, the bowl shattered.

I looked over at my father, who I knew would be very angry. In this case, however, he looked at Johnny with incredulity: "What's wrong with you?" he said with a face that managed surprise, disappointment, and sternness at the same time. I must have blocked any punishment meted out, but I can imagine that my father escorted Johnny inside roughly. Had I done something like that, the punishment would have been swift, with hard whacks on the behind, followed by days of forced inactivity. However, Johnny was a visitor and the son of my father's brother-in-law. So the rules of hospitality may have preserved Johnny's hind end.

This extraordinary event notwithstanding, we spent most of our time doing ordinary things: playing football or baseball, roasting hot dogs or

Vienna sausages over an open pit fire in the backyard, and going to movies or swimming.

Aside from visiting cousins, we sometimes went to Aunt Bebe's camp in Hackberry, Louisiana. Aunt Bebe, pronounced "BB," was my mother's older sister. By today's standards she and her husband (Uncle Lee) were not extremely wealthy. By mid-1960s standards, however, they were set. They owned a large, rambling home in Sulphur, Louisiana, just west of Lake Charles, and they also owned Breaux's Crescent Drugs, an independent pharmacy that provided a high standard of living. We'd sometimes meet at their store, pick out candy bars, chocolate covered peanuts, or other treats, and one of them would follow us to their home less than a mile away.

We liked going to her house because in the garage was a real drink machine. Uncle Ed had his slot machine; Aunt Bebe had a drink machine! Feed it a dime, and it dispensed eight-ounce bottles of soft drinks, cold enough to hurt your teeth on hot summer days. Mom trained us well—we could not ask for one before the obligatory hellos, kisses, and small talk. It was up to Aunt Bebe to ask us if we wanted a bottle, and she often provided the coins.

After a stop at the house, we'd pile back into the Ford Wagon and head to Hackberry, south of Lake Charles and Sulphur, about halfway between them and the coastal waters of the Gulf of Mexico. There, we set up at the camp, which sat on banks of the Calcasieu River and ship channel. This second home, although "just" a camp in nondescript Hackberry, reinforced to us that Aunt Bebe and Uncle Lee were well off. Not many people we knew had vacation homes in those days. It was an extravagance! Not just the camp itself, but their two boats—a fiberglass speedboat and a flat-bottomed aluminum skiff—both with outboard motors. For kids from southwest Louisiana, this was as good as it got!

We spent days cane-pole fishing, floating on inner tubes, swimming in the muddy water, crabbing and boating. Mom always brought some frozen chicken necks to use as crab bait. She would tie a neck and some weights onto a line, drop it off the pier into the murky water, and wait. This line-method of crabbing required great skill and patience. Mom taught us to pull the line up very slowly and smoothly, and when we felt a crab nibbling on the neck, to sink a long-handled net quietly behind the line in the water. When the munching crab became the least bit visible, you had to move the net carefully under and around the crab, let the crab and neck sink softly into the net and then pull the net up quickly—with the line, weights, chicken neck, and crab in it. She had mastered this technique over the years. Several crabs darted to their freedom before I got the knack of it.

A far easier method, and one that often yielded more than a single crab, was to tie the chicken neck to the bottom of a crab trap. The trap had two metal rings covered in netting. The line on the pier attached to four lines spaced at ninety degrees on the upper metal ring. When the trap hit the bottom of the river, it lay flat. Crabs came for their dinner, as they did with the open-line method, but the technique here was opposite. Instead of a slow, gentle drawing of the line, the trick with the trap was to pull the line straight up as fast as possible. That way any dining crabs would be surrounded by the sides of the trap, jerked up by the quick pull, and held in place by the force of the upward-travelling basket.

The camp came supplied with a semi-submersible large metal-screened basket. Its top stood above the water line. We'd dump the live crabs in to the basket, throw in a few chicken necks so they could "fatten" up, and wait until we had several dozen for a live, fresh crab boil. I learned to crack open crabs and extract their sweet meat before I learned golf.

When we weren't crabbing, we were fishing. No rods and reels, just cane poles with red and white floats on the line about three or four feet above the weights and the hook. My mother loved fried catfish, and catfish were plentiful in the Calcasieu River. We used sliced hot dogs or small frozen shrimp for bait, set the floats and waited for a hit. When the float went under, we jerked the pole up. I was too young and squeamish to remove a fish from the hook, so I'd take my catches to Mom or Dad for removal. My mother once put her rubber-thonged foot on the back of a catfish to keep it still while removing the hook. When she did, the fish shot its dorsal fin straight up. Needle like, it penetrated the rubber thong and went into the bottom of her foot—a scary situation requiring a bit of medical attention. Snagged catfish shared the screen basket with the crabs until they were gathered with nets, cleaned, and fried.

I think my mother liked fishing and crabbing because they required waiting and watching, activities I see now as associated with the spiritual life, a sort of between space. Waiting and watching require patience, which was fostered in my stoic mother, I think, by many childhood upheavals—her father's alcoholism and abandonment, frequent moves, the loss of her younger sister to polio. I don't know what she wondered about while crabbing or fishing, but I remember her enthusiasm, and I wanted to feel what I thought she felt.

Recollections on a Road Between

Fishing and crabbing slowed her down, gave her time, and I see them now as types of memory. Some have to be coaxed slowly and gently, as though softly tugging on a line. Some bobble at the surface and need to be snagged like a fish with a quick jerk. Some wander into the web of consciousness and are easily retrieved.

Because the river was also part of a ship channel, large tankers or cargo ships often sailed down from Lake Charles to the Gulf. My sisters, Debbie especially, loved floating out on her inner tube to ride the ships' wakes. In my memory now, she seemed to get perilously close to them. Debbie would wave to the shipmates on deck who often waved back, happy for the distraction of an attractive young woman! On the fishing pier, we'd make a signal for the ship to sound its horn, and the captain often obliged. What fun to communicate with sailors on their way with cargo to who knew where!

I was too small to go far out on an inner tube, but I recall paddling with Mike and Debbie in the aluminum skiff to Mud Island, a small barrier island between the ship channel and Calcasieu Lake. The island was aptly named, because once on its shore, mud pits grabbed your feet, making it difficult to walk and giving the sense of sinking deeply into the muck, like explorers (or more often their guides) in movies who were slowly swallowed by quicksand.

My imagination sometimes got the better of me. Would I sink so far that, like the hapless characters on TV, I'd be lost to the grime? Although we didn't sink much beyond our shins or knees, it seemed deeper. The mud was a mess, drying quickly on the skin in the sun—and it had a greasy consistency not easily cleaned off. Debbie and Mike played a game with the mud, sinking one foot into it with just enough air and water to create very loud, gurgling farts. We laughed hysterically, especially when they did it in imitation of our grandmother, Ma'malle, whose gastro-intestinal tract seemed perpetually filled with gas.

As I've said, Mike had curly hair and shiny braces on his teeth. We teased him mercilessly, nicknamed him "Curls and Coils," which we chanted whenever we wanted to get the better of him, which he didn't like. At home in Lafayette, he began wearing old stockings on his head to try to straighten his hair. We teased him for that too, though once he scared Harvey so badly in this get up, my father told him the stocking was "affecting the blood flow to his brain."

Mike also tended to sleep walk. One night at Aunt BeBe's camp, we awakened to terrifying screams. Debbie roused, and found a contorted face near her in the dim light. Someone turned on the lights to find Mike, pulling a stocking from his head. He had got the better of us in his sleep. At least he told us he was asleep.

Fear, or the imagined threat of it, seemed a fraternal twin to the memories of my travels as a youth. Although travel as an adult has been more exotic, it has sometimes been more scripted and less spontaneous. The thrill of a simple mud pit, the soft tug of a crab line, and the succulence of a fresh crab boil seem small compared to a walk inside the Grand Mosque in Abu Dhabi or a trip to Oman, yet the memories helped me find out more—about myself, my family, our place in the social hierarchy of south Louisiana, and about memory itself.

⌒

Years later, after Jan and I had our own kids, we'd often spend time at my sister Jerrie's bay house on Galveston Island. Mom and Dad would meet us there, and we'd crab and fish in the dark waters of Galveston Bay. Small rods and reels replaced the old cane poles, and jet skis stood in for the old boats. But my mother taught our kids how to cast, to wait, to watch the float, and to be patient.

Was she remembering her sister's camp in Hackberry? Was she remembering her childhood, her early years of marriage, her father, her mother? While she had not read St. Augustine, I wonder if she felt the tug of his great "subterranean shrine" of memory.

Who knows where memory resides? I am continually surprised at my experience of memory.

I may be walking down a busy city street, and a memory of golf or a movie or a comment from my parents might pop into my consciousness. I may be eating with friends, and I remember playing the game *Risk* as a youth or an image of Montepulciano, Italy, or an exceptional four-iron shot I hit while playing golf in Alexandria, Louisiana. *Why now? Why here? What's the connection? Is there a connection?*

Neuroscientists do well to study the brain in search of a place or region where memory might reside, but it seems to me that memory suffuses a person, not just his or her brain. It shapes the person who remembers just as much as a person shapes the memories he or she recollects. Memory extends like the infinite regress of the ripples caused by a float hitting the water. Some are easily retrieved; some need a quick jerk or a gentle tug—like fishing and crabbing on the Calcasieu River at Aunt Bebe's camp.

3

Nothing remains but desire and desire comes howling down Elysian Fields like a mistral.

—WALKER PERCY, *THE MOVIEGOER*

I REMEMBER A TRIP to False River near New Roads, Louisiana. False River is a wide, deep, and calm oxbow lake of the Mississippi. My mother's brother, Uncle Ed, had a friend who had a camp on the river, and he invited me and Mike to the camp with him and some of his kids for a weekend. We fished for perch from a small pier, pan-fried them for breakfast, water-skied, and took out a small flat-bottom boat to fish further out in the river.

One beautiful late-spring or early summer day, with the morning light soft, and the gentlest of breezes crossing the water, Mike and I went out with Uncle Ed in the small boat. The calm waters of the river reflected a soft, dull-blue sky, a morning sky just before the sun rises. It seemed we had the river to ourselves, although in the distance from time to time, another boat glided mutely across its glass-like surface. Uncle Ed brought a small transistor radio with him, and began to sing along with Helen Reddy's yearning and melancholic version of "Delta Dawn," quietly, as though not to disrupt the morning calm.

In the morning light on the calm river, Reddy's voice and Uncle Ed's soft singing seemed at once distant and very near, outside me but also inside. A deep rush of something, I didn't know what, overcame me, something mournful and happy, something that made me want more of whatever it was—desire, longing, a found loss, a lost fullness.

Recollections on a Road Between

Much later, as a student in Rome, I took trips to the French Alps during Christmas break to meet friends from the seminary in Louvain, Belgium. We skied, one year in Tignes, the next year in Les Arcs. On the way back from Les Arcs, I had not made a reservation for a sleeper car, and though I knew I shouldn't board a train composed entirely of sleeper cars, I did anyway, tapping into a type of magical thinking that would insinuate itself into my consciousness from time to time. *Surely, no one will care that I'm on the train—perhaps a couchette will open; the conductor won't find me; if nothing opens up, I can just sit in the hallway.*

It so happened that I met a young woman on this train who thought, like me, that she would not be found out. We talked in the hallway. She was a graduate student in Russian studies at one of the Ivy League schools. Had this been a movie, this encounter would have been the "meet cute." Two young people traveling Europe during the holidays meet on a train neither should be on in the first place. The script might have played out so that they have some sort of sexual encounter.

It is true I was filled with desire, but I was also wracked by a paralysis because of my "pre-priestly" status. So the script played out differently. The conductor found us (how could he not?), and in the middle of the night, he forced us off the train in Milan. We walked a few blocks to the snow-covered piazza near the historic cathedral and waited for a train due later in the morning, which the conductor told us we could board legitimately.

We talked of our lives, tried to keep each other warm in the cold winter night by covering ourselves with our coats, but we were both self-conscious. I was awed by her study of Russian at a top-notch university. She could not understand my studies for a priestly life. So, we sat until the sun rose, walked back to the train station, and caught the next train to Rome. My spiritual director, Larry, met us at the station in his Fiat 124, gave her a ride back to her hostel, and took me back to the North American College with him. I never saw her or heard from her again. Not exactly the stuff of romance.

This unlikely script played out several times during my time as a seminarian. I often had a deep desire for what I knew I couldn't have, and I looked at myself in whatever mirror I found before me and wondered if I could really become a priest. I found myself between the desire to become a priest and more "secular" desires.

Was this a simple "grass is greener" phenomenon, a fear of commitment, a lack of fortitude, a plea for attention, a flaw in character, "normal" desire? I don't know. The seminary tended to exacerbate sexual desire, but sometimes I just wanted to be noticed.

⁓

In seventh- or eighth-grade at my Catholic school in Lafayette, desires of all sorts arose.

Once, I set off a "booby trap" in class for no particular reason. It was a firework with strings at its ends that you secured with tacks—one end on a door and the other on the door's frame. When an unsuspecting victim opened the door, the strings stretched and set off the charge. I pulled the two strings in class. For this offense I got a lesson in Kantian ethics. Sent to the Principal's office, Brother Patrick asked, "What if everyone did that?" The question struck me as illogical. Of course, everyone would *not* do that. I had little understanding of ethical systems, however.

I remember an open reading session in Sr. Rigali's class. Most of my classmates remained at their desks, but I lay down on my stomach on a book case in the back of the room. It must have looked as though I was engaged in a vulgar act as one of the girls got Sr. Rigali's attention to say with disgust, "Look at Eddie!" She clucked her tongue and told me to get down. In fourth grade, Mrs. Trahan invited to class a young officer who had just returned from Vietnam. I can't remember what he talked about, but I do remember raising my hand to ask, "Did you know that if you drink beer through a straw, you'll get drunk?" I had heard my brothers talking about this earlier in the week and the idea fascinated me. Clearly, I was out of line. Did these odd acts mimic my rolling down the stairs at the house in New Orleans? A desire to be noticed?

When we moved back to New Orleans in 1972, I attended a public school for the first time. Aside from the episodes of bullying I described earlier, I also knew happiness.

In homeroom we sat in alphabetical order, and I had the good fortune of sitting next to Carol, a beautiful, blue-eyed blond, with a beaming smile, enhanced by a pretty nose and an intelligent forehead. Much more mature physically than my five-foot four inches and 110 pounds, Carol played along with my foolishness. I'd joke with her in the mornings during roll call.

In my best Cary Grant voice, I might say, "There's only one thing separating us, Carol."

"What's that?" she would ask.

"This leg on the desk."

It's an early instance of a corny "dad" joke, something I'd "perfect" years later, to the chagrin of Jan and the kids. Carol would laugh politely, though not, I thought, dishonestly. There was no question of dating, for she was, I thought, beyond me, and I was too shaky and insecure for even the possibility of asking.

I can't remember if my mother gave me a talk about sex before ninth grade (upon entering public school) or before I began tenth grade. I'm pretty sure it was the former. And I don't remember many details of that talk. I do remember her saying, however, that married men and women liked "rubbing and touching one another all over" and that sex led to babies. And I remember asking fearfully and earnestly, "But how do you actually do it?" When she told me, I was perplexed but intrigued.

As though to make up for her frank description, she opened the drawer of her bedside table and gave me an old book with yellowed pages titled *Listen, Son: Twelve Heart-to-Heart Talks of a Father to His Son*. I took it to my room, read a few pages, and put it away. I don't think I ever looked at it again. A Catholic manual on sex and procreation published in 1952, it no doubt helped many young boys understand their growing urges, but I was turned off by the tone, a pietistic sanctimoniousness that annoys me to this day. Copies can still be found on Amazon.

I found my mother's frankness more appealing.

I had crushes on girls at school in Lafayette. And I had attended parties there, mostly supervised, where we danced, played spin the bottle (not to kiss but for choosing dance partners). But I was nowhere near comfortable in my growing awareness of sexuality.

I recall a party in Lafayette that made me uncomfortable and puzzled, but aroused and pensive at the same time. This one took place at classmate's house several miles outside the city on a large plot of land (ten acres?) with a big two-story farm house set back a few hundred yards from a country road. Dancing, punch, sandwiches, and chips—and little supervision, if any—made this party feel "grown-up."

At one point, I was urged by friends to take a look upstairs. There I saw one of the more "mature" girls from our class sitting in a chair with another classmate beside her. Some friends used to make crude jokes I pretended to understand because she already had well-developed breasts and a small waist that broadened into an ample hips and legs. I remember her surprise at seeing me. She looked at me directly and, I thought, invitingly. Earlier, I found that through friends that she "liked" me, something they teased me about mercilessly. I had no clue as to why, and I couldn't imagine myself "going out" with her, or with anyone for that matter. Standing in her presence in the upstairs room at the party, I didn't know what I felt—mostly awkward and afraid. Those eyes offered…I didn't know what.

A few weeks later, a friend told me that at the party in the upstairs room, the boy sitting next to her on the chair had his hand up her skirt. I had a vague idea of what that meant, but I was too ashamed of my inexperience and too afraid of the image to ask.

The memory found its way into a poem I wrote many years later for a project of photographs and poems I was working on with a friend. I offer it here:

At the Threshold

I remember a daily pre-class ritual
carried on with friends in seventh grade.
Two or three of us sat on some old
concrete steps and two or three others
stood facing them such that whatever
might be going on behind or to the side
could still be seen.

It sounds so simple—four to six kids
(male, Catholic) killing time,
talking about last night's ball game
or today's test or tomorrow's party at
a friend's, an easy life really, no doubt
duplicated many times over—
a kind of shell.

But there was the science teacher who
drank too much, too often, and slept
off the booze in class; there was the guy
whose voice seemed a bit too feminine,

and the girl whose body made you
wonder what she meant when she
looked right into your eyes; and there was
a new sort of banter, daring but
dimly known; and there was always that
basement storeroom—the janitors' office,
we smirked—next to our steps and
locked; they would emerge from time to time
smelly and wearied.

I have often wanted to go back to see
if my memory is playing games or
not. Is that door to the left as I recall it?
Were the steps at the corner of the
building, or were they set back?
And where is Danny, or Dean, or
Stevie? Would they recall our being
there—straining not to show the strain
of easy lives in quiet pain?

The memory of the party converted first to a poem, later to narrative, now here part of my story, and part of your experience of my story. I think the poem occupies, like memory, an interstitial place, Augustine's subterranean shrine rippling outward to unfathomable ends. Note the title—"At the Threshold"—an in-between, liminal space.

I attended O. Perry Walker High School in New Orleans. There, my place was as insider/outsider—"between." I wasn't a jock, but I hung out with a fellow who was the football team captain (the OPW Chargers), played middle linebacker, and dated the homecoming queen, a universally recognized beauty among most boys at the school.

I liked sports, but didn't play for OPW. I played basketball in the hot New Orleans nights with an eclectic group of classmates, played golf with friends at Bayou Barriere Country Club or Brechtel Park, and played pickup touch football games at the elementary school down the street or in the street in front of our house. I also picked up table tennis because of an older friend, he a former seminarian, and played it seriously for several years.

Some of these fellows read Ayn Rand, whom I had not heard of, listened to Yes, Pink Floyd, or Jethro Tull, and knew already they wanted to study architecture or electrical engineering or law. One fellow donned the costume of the Charger mascot each week at football games and rode a unicycle up and down the home-field sideline revving up the crowd. I did not get involved in clubs at school, except for a very brief stint with the yearbook.

**With John around the time of my High School graduation.
New Orleans, LA, May, 1976.**

I took honors, but not AP biology, which was reserved for wanna-be doctors, took honors Algebra II and Trigonometry, but not Calculus, like the future engineers. I dated "in" girls but also "out" girls. With the "in" girls I always felt I had to live up to something I wasn't. But I didn't possess any more ease with "out" girls.

I took an "in girl," Barbara, to senior prom, though she was a junior and on crutches because she had a recent knee injury. She was smart, and many boys considered her desirable. At school, I watched her from a distance, liked her bobbed blond hair, and what I saw as her spunky character. Although I didn't really know her, I asked her to prom, mostly because I was tired of feeling "out" and wanted to feel "in."

She couldn't dance because of her injured leg, though she allowed me to prop her up on one side—a crutch on the other—while we moved around the dance floor. We didn't really talk much to one another and I felt as though I was watching myself from above, while others were watching me, especially when we went to an "after-party" with ten or twelve friends in a room in a downtown hotel. We sat against the wall, her injured leg outstretched, and I don't remember anything else about that evening except dropping her off at the end of the night to visit another "in" girl, very smart, and who I thought was destined for great things and on whom I had an old-fashioned crush. How odd!

⁌

I had a job after school and on weekends as the receptionist at the Mary Joseph Residence, an old-folks home run by the Little Sisters of the Poor and walking distance from our house. I walked or rode my bike to work most days, but on some days my parents came together to pick me up. I'd wait for them outside the automatic doors leading to the lobby. Once, as I settled into the back seat, my dad told me with pride that I looked like "an all-American boy" standing there.

I didn't quite know what he meant, although images of white teeth, nice hair, good looks, "success," and good morals (all gleaned from television and sports) popped into my head. I was happy for what I knew was a compliment, though I felt a sense of pretense as well—his image of me did not match my image of myself. Even then, I wasn't sure I wanted to be "all American," although I was glad for my father's approval.

My shift covered 4:30 to 8:00 p.m., and I was relieved by night security. One fellow, a black man about thirty years old, stuttered helplessly. He shook his head, contorted his mouth, began, got snagged, and tried again. I did my best to let him finish his sentences, not always successfully. Still today, I struggle with allowing people to finish their thoughts, even those who don't stutter. To my mind, the speech impediment made him a kind man, though I don't recall what sort of character he was.

I do know he was not like the other guard, a white man with crooked teeth who boasted of sleeping with a black nurse from the skilled-care unit: "You ain't had nothing till you've had that sweet dark meat." I listened with an attitude between moral superiority—only a "lowlife" would have sex on the job—and guilty desire—conjuring an image of this fellow in bed with the nurse. Was this the way folks got along in the world?

A few years after the "sex" talk from my mother, I entered a period of adolescent experimentations on myself, which made me feel guilty. I had not had sex as some of my classmates had. I remember a friend who used to join us sometimes for Friday-night basketball saying he enjoyed the "fringe benefits of marriage" without the marriage. This news surprised me. What he told me seemed so "grown up." I could never have done that, much less told anyone about it, though I didn't dare let on to how I felt.

Sex was everywhere in the 1970s. National Airlines commercials used it to sell flights, naming their planes after women: "I'm Judy," a series of commercials went, "Fly me!" A Gillette commercial featured a sultry woman telling her man when he shaved to "Take it off; take it all off." And an early feminist commercial showed a lusty business-woman singing, "I can bring home the bacon, fry it up in a pan, and never, never, ever let you forget you're a man, 'cause I'm a woooman."

I was a young guilt-ridden man, and the guilt became a problem for me. What the culture portrayed about women and sex and what I was expected to live up to as a child of my parents and a Catholic didn't mesh very well. Nevertheless, we watched the commercials with little or no comment.

I knew a little about hypnotism from my cousin, a psychiatrist, because he used to give demonstrations of it using his children as subjects. I convinced myself that if I were hypnotized, I could overcome what I thought was a problem I had with my adolescent experimentations. One day, while working at the receptionist's desk, I waited until no one was around, and I called the office of a psychiatrist to ask, very quietly, if it were possible to hypnotize someone over the phone. The voice on the other end must have thought I was nuts. She invited me to come into the office for a consultation. No way was I going to go into an office! I felt more embarrassed than before I called. I quickly hung up the phone.

A few more days of fretting, and finally, I called our parish priest, Father Roy, and asked to meet with him.

Fr. Roy was a canny Cajun from New Roads, Louisiana. Pious, but down-to-earth; earnest, but with a good sense of humor; buoyant and mildly rebellious; someone who had a long battle with pemphigus—an autoimmune disease, which I think deepened his spirituality and forced him to accept limitations. Fr. Roy also had a practiced mnemonic device that allowed him to remember a name after having met a person just once. He reinforced his memory by using each person's name when they received communion: "Eddie, the Body of Christ," which opened a personal connection immediately and added to the vibrancy of the parish and the personal relationships he fostered.

Because it was new, the parish leased the chapel at Our Lady of Holy Cross College while its own church building was planned and constructed. (In the year 2000, I became Senior Vice President for Academic Affairs at that college.)

I rode my bike to Fr. Roy's office next to the chapel at Our Lady of Holy Cross. He welcomed me and asked me what was on my mind. I don't remember what I said. I was nervous and probably stammered and spoke in half sentences. He interrupted me at one point and said, "Are you worried about masturbation?" *Wow!* I thought. *How could he know this, and why was a priest telling me my own fears about THIS subject?*

But he was right, and, like a penitent, a huge weight lifted from me. He told me that it was "normal," that the stories people told of hair growing on your palms were not true (I had not heard such stories), and that though he understood my feelings, there was no reason to berate myself about it. That meeting began a relationship with him and the parish that eventually led to my decision to enter the seminary in the fall of 1977—after a year of studies in engineering at LSU.

I don't mean to draw a straight line from being relieved about learning my adolescent sexual practice was "normal" to entry into the seminary, but rather Fr. Roy's sense of compassion, his down-to-earth approach, his taking the time to hear me without judgment, without even my having to say much, made a connection for me and showed me priesthood could be an option. If he could relieve me of such a burden, wouldn't it be good for me to do the same for others?

From the time of that meeting, he began suggesting I consider the seminary as a college option, though he stood back enough to give me space as well. I had no idea what I wanted, but Fr. Roy showed the possibility of a direction, and his suggestion fortified the memories of my mother's religiosity, her association with the Marianites and the Grey Nuns, the Christian Brothers who ran the Catholic School in Lafayette, the many visitors my sisters brought back to Lafayette after they first moved to Houston, and even my namesake, Fr. Ed Templeton, whose photo at my baptism remains seared in my memory.

After my talk with Fr. Roy, I had more confidence in myself and began to feel more at ease in my interactions with girls. I remember vividly a classmate who had moved away from our neighborhood after her junior year because her father was transferred out of state for his work. She returned for a visit and stayed with a mutual friend who lived down the street from us. She and I went out. She confessed that she had the "hugest crush" on me and that she was sorry she had had to leave. I had never thought someone could feel this way about me! We "parked." I eventually unbuttoned her blouse—she had invited my doing so!—and we enjoyed adolescent lust. We did not "have sex," though it was the closest thing to it. Overcome, I feared and reveled in lack of control.

I was also attracted to a classmate with whom I had not given much thought because she was dating a football player. I assumed they were inseparable. Although she worked at Mary Joseph Residence, our interactions were mainly a quick hello as she walked by the receptionist's desk in her white kitchen uniform to clock-in for her shift. One night, I don't remember how we arranged it, she asked to see me at my home. I said sure. When she arrived, she took me to the side of our house and told me she really liked me. We engaged in serious kissing. "What about Hank?" I asked. She didn't mind, though she did say, with some satisfaction, that he would not like her doing what she was doing.

After that first night, she stopped by the house several more times. I thought my mother knew nothing about it, but one day, she teased me (with some pride, I thought) about my "kissing that blonde girl on the side of the house." I was relieved that my mother thought this was "normal" behavior, especially because I enjoyed it so much!

Recollections on a Road Between

~

Aside from these new escapades, I remember lying flat on my back in bed for hours—just thinking, allowing my mind to wander. I'd wonder about my future. *What would I do?* For a time, I'd imitate news anchors thinking I'd become a national reporter: "This is Eddie Dupuy for ABC News." I thought about flying or becoming an astronaut. I thought about my place in the family or at school—and even in the universe. *What's it all about, Alfie?*—Andy Williams' version, a song my mother played endlessly on her large stereo.

Sometimes I'd think about Fr. Roy's suggestion that I study for the priesthood, feeling I had been tapped to do something extraordinary. Sometimes I despaired of ever finding my way. I'd listen to music with headphones I'd purchased with my savings from work. Not Yes or Jethro Tull, but James Taylor, Neil Diamond, Jim Croce, Simon and Garfunkel, the Beatles. I played them so often I can still remember the lyrics: "I am I said, and no one heard at all, not even the chair."

What did I desire? Company, attention, approval, place, a sense of purpose, a feeling of being?

~

I graduated thirty-fifth in a class of about 630 students from O. Perry Walker. I remember the ranking not only because it was on my final transcript but because most of my older siblings were either valedictorian or salutatorian of their classes, and I felt the pressure of living up to their standards. Whereas all of my family before me had attended the University of Louisiana at Lafayette, I decided to follow in my father's footsteps and attend LSU. I would study not petroleum engineering but mechanical engineering.

I don't recall any conscious discernment regarding this track. I was good at math, enjoyed the physics class during my senior year at OPW, and I was interested in the ways things worked—taking apart a Cox .049 engine in Lafayette, for example, or planning to build a telescope, a project I explored for weeks but which I eventually scrapped because of the high price of lenses.

My mother always thought I'd be the handyman in the family. Though an engineer, my father was not good with building or fixing things. I had a little of that knack, and I wanted to go a slightly different route from my family—an indication, perhaps, of our continued competition.

Not long before I left for LSU, I met with Fr. Roy. He wished me good luck, but took the opportunity to remind me that he thought the priesthood still might be something for me to consider.

My mom drove me to Baton Rouge and helped me move into my room at Hatcher Hall. René deLaup, a high-school classmate who about eight years later introduced me to Jan, would be my roommate. When my mom left, I felt liberated and sad, a mix I didn't quite understand. I'm pretty sure I was in a minority of students, who feeling that way, walked over to the Catholic Student Center for solace. It wasn't long, however, before a sense of liberty replaced the cloak of sadness, and I got into the spirit (and flesh) of college life.

My scholastic performance that first year reflected an unconscious desire for what today might be called the "meritocracy." I believed that hard work (assiduous study) would bring me "success," defined as a good job with a good salary and a stable life. I took copious notes on pages of loose-leaf paper, which I numbered and placed into a file. I went to the library after classes nearly every day to review the notes. I used this system through college and grad school.

Proud to get an "A" in most classes, I managed only a "B" in calculus, the concepts of which stumped me. But I enjoyed my "success" on a route to what I thought I wanted. I also think, however, that I experienced stirrings of something else: an enthusiasm and awakening of the pleasure of learning for learning's sake, not just for grades, but for something "large and unknown," though I didn't know what.

I had glimpses of this sort of desire when I took an introductory geology class. After our move to New Orleans in 1972, we took a long road trip up to see my sister Polly and her husband, Jim, and my first nephew—my parents' first grandchild, in Calgary, Alberta, Canada. I loved the mountains and the clear running rivers, so different from the dark waters of the Calcasieu River or the muddy Mississippi. Since Jim was a geophysicist, he could point out and name features of the landscape. The geology class at LSU reinforced his off-hand lectures.

I was swept up in the section on physical geology, the difference between U- and V-shaped valleys, the relatively quick work of rivers and the slow work of glaciers carving the landscape and leaving behind moraines, lakes, cirques, and drumlin hills. The latter two names held for me almost incantatory powers.

I found great excitement in an Intro to Sociology course, awakened for the first time to hidden power of groups. Later, Max Weber's writings on sociology and religion, the "charismatic leader" whose vision unites followers, the original charism passed on and eventually so unrecognizably transformed that a new leader emerges to correct the course.

I loved my mechanical drawing class, the strict rules for depicting iron, or stainless steel, or aluminum along with the varying grades of pencils used to depict complicated machinery. The T-bar, scale-ruler, and triangles—this was the time before CAD—became magical tools for a while, and I felt like Shakespeare's Prospero as I oversaw the drawings I made.

The tools, the rules of their use, the names of things physical and social—these awakened in me a sense of longing, a desire to know more, to name more, perhaps even an inchoate desire to name myself through memory and narrative, as I try to do now, here.

I don't remember exactly how it started, but the sense of longing I began to feel turned into sadness, which deepened longing, which is how longing works. You sense something beyond you that elicits happiness, and you think it will always make you happy, but its capture continually eludes you, or if captured, proves to be less than what you expected, which makes you sad, thereby longing for more. And so the cycle of happiness/sadness, the mixture of the two, goes around and around.

I think this is what I had first experienced on that quiet morning on False River as Uncle Ed sang with Helen Reddy.

Perhaps it was the relative lack of success in Calculus that scared me. Or maybe it was the joy I felt in opening new vistas (geology, sociology, mechanical drawing). Maybe I needed affirmation from my parents, Fr. Roy, and others. Maybe it was all those hours I lay on my bed thinking about the future. Maybe it was the kindness of Fr. Roy or the nuns whom my mother befriended or the friends my sisters brought back from Houston. Or maybe God stirred this longing and was also its object. I think it was all of the above. A "call" to priesthood does not drop out of thin air, despite St. Paul's thunderous conversion. It is rooted in life—now, here—in history.

At some point in the spring semester at LSU, I decided I would enter the seminary in the fall. My friend Chris, who lived next door, listened to me as I went through the decision process and recalls my telling him, "Somebody's got to do it. Why not me?"—or something like that. Ah, ego!

My decision seemed at once opaque and right. Becoming a priest seemed the summation of my life to that point, something "honorary," something different, and something mysterious, something attractive yet fearful. To say one feels called by God can be an ego boost, despite the prophets, who complained to God when called as being too sinful or too stupid or too ineloquent to accept his call. Maybe they're right. If God calls, you should run, hide, say thanks but no thanks!

I felt something like that too. When in the first year of seminary I read Rudolph Otto's classic, *The Idea of the Holy*, and encountered his description of the *mysterium tremendum*—the holy at once attractive and dreadful—I knew in my bones what he meant.

Whatever the cause, whatever story I might tell, the fact is that I left LSU to attend Saint Joseph Seminary College, colloquially called "St. Ben." My decision left a strong enough impression on Chris, my next-door neighbor, that six years later when I had decided to leave the seminary (again full of longing and dread), he called me in Rome out of the blue to tell me he had decided to enter the Jesuits. He also told me that he remembered our conversations back at LSU.

4

Horatio: O day and night, but this is wondrous strange!

Hamlet: And therefore as a stranger give it welcome. There are more things in Heaven and on Earth, Horatio, than are dreamt of in your philosophy.

–*Hamlet*, I.v.163–167

Father Roy proudly drove me to Saint Joseph Seminary College in late August of 1977. He delighted that one of his parishioners, one in whom he had fostered a potential vocation, now took the steps necessary to explore that call. To mark my entry into the seminary, he gave me a Bible inscribed with a heartfelt, theologically-centered message, one I read so many times I nearly had it memorized. I still have the bible with the message:

> Dear Ed:
>
> With this "Word of God in words of man," I pledge my prayer, my help, and my best wishes to you as you enter this new chapter in your own journey to the Father. Holy Spirit Parish is behind and with you.
>
> May your way be rich in music, beauty, and new life's growth: Emmanuel.
>
> It is a privilege to be your friend.
> Allen Roy

Reading this message now, after years of reading the Word of God and the words of men and women, I am struck at its depth and simplicity. The Bible is not a transcription of the Word of God, but an historical document, a story developed in time, by the hands and memories of individuals and communities. And my life at St. Ben was a new chapter not only in the journey of my life, which it certainly was, but also in the life of the communal church. His declaration of parity, of friendship, furthermore, indicated an unusual respect for a shaky nineteen-year-old trying to find his way.

I had been to St. Ben several times because my mom had a cousin, Br. Steve, who was a monk there. The monks run the college at the Abbey. Our family visited Br. Steve from time to time, and we had picnics or played on the Abbey's sprawling, beautiful, land.

The Abbey grounds consist of about 1200 acres, only a few of which are cleared for the abbey and seminary college complex and some pastures. The remaining acres comprise a vast pine forest. We'd walk the grounds dotted with azaleas and dogwoods, old "holy" oaks—ferns growing on their thick branches—a tributary of the Bogue Falaya, cattle pastures, pine forest, and two small lakes. And of course we'd attend Mass.

My trip with Fr. Roy, however, held a gravity that those visits didn't. Here was I, Eddie Dupuy, "All-American Boy," going down a track that seemed counter to what most of America was about. I enjoyed the affirmation of Fr. Roy, the pride of my parents, and the welcome of the monastic faculty. And I found it reassuring that the path, though not heavily trodden, was not overgrown. The decision seemed both consonant with and different from the steps I had taken up to this point.

"Why would you do a thing like that," a friend asked? "It seems so final."

I couldn't easily answer or reconcile my own competing views. Nor could I foresee the openness, imbalance, and disruption that awaited me.

I remember sitting in the church, sun shining through the rose window, illuminating the murals of Dom Gregory de Witt with a warm glow. I remember the lakes beside the Abbey Church, so still that the image of the church and the large oak at its side rested, unperturbed, on its surface. I remember the smell of fresh cow dung in the pastures, gassy and grassy. I remember the acrid smell of the old chemistry lab I cleaned out to use as a dark room when I was yearbook editor. I remember hiking down the Bogue Falaya when it was low, sand and pebbles squishing through my toes. I remember a lesson from a visiting monk about Heraclitus' stream—and another about the moon as the reflection of a greater glory. I remember walking through the Abbey cemetery, conscious of St. Benedict's admonition to "keep death daily before your eyes."

The bucolic grounds fostered meditation, and prompted in me a desire to write. I wrote my first poems at St. Ben, typed on index cards. I also wrote a story based on the classic hero's journey with a dose of spirituality—about "Seeker," a leaf on a tree and his attempt to "let go" of his familiar life, connected to the tree, for the unknown that fall might bring, all early instances of grappling with the imbalance, the openness, and intensity of seminary life.

Saint Joseph Abbey Church, Saint Benedict, LA.
I began studies at Saint Joseph Seminary College in fall of 1977.

To say that "intensity" characterizes that time doesn't really clarify the experience. In one of her letters to Betty Hester, Flannery O'Connor writes, and I paraphrase here, that "most people have no idea what goes on in a seminary. And if they knew they would likely be shocked." O'Connor takes seriously the fact that the church is built on a communion of saints who are sinners. She calls it a "communion created upon human imperfection... created from what we make of our grotesque state."

If you place a hundred or so young men who feel called by God (with all the ambiguities that entails), and put them in a community under the supervision of monks who live in community, the usual human shortcomings that communities foster magnify (competition, jealously, rivalry, pettiness, ambition, judgment) along with exaggerations of their obverse (passiveness, over-concern, support, hesitation at making judgments, excessive piety). The intensity of the life requires a delicate stance, one that wavers the between the two extremes. Some did well at holding the extremes in tension, while others drifted to one pole or the other. I did both.

My entry into the seminary altered my history, but it did not abolish it. Still fiercely competitive, I played basketball, tennis, table tennis, and football, which provided a sense of camaraderie—and rivalry. There was a fellow whom I just did not like, and I remember scuffles with him on the football field. I tracked him down on kickoffs only to knock him to the ground. We didn't have to get along, but we couldn't forget about one another either.

The intensity of seminary life came about also because of formation. The military has basic training; seminary has formation. Like training, formation fosters a set of skills and practices designed to serve as a foundation for future priests—prayer, scripture reading, Mass attendance, discernment, and self-reflection. Based on a set of broad guidelines promulgated by the bishops' conference of the United States and ratified by Rome, formation emphasizes the human, spiritual, intellectual, pastoral, and communal dimensions of the priestly life. A seminarian chooses (or is assigned) a spiritual director, for example, with whom a human relationship develops to discuss the seminarian's prayer life, his progress in classes, his work beyond the classroom (serving in a parish, for example), and his contributions to the communal life of the seminary.

Each year, each seminarian goes through an evaluation that is based on these broad areas of formation. The spiritual director attends, but does not contribute to the formation committee's assessment of the student. The evaluation becomes the basis for future one-to-one discussions between a seminarian and his spiritual director. One was consistently checking himself—or felt that he should have been.

Formation took place outside the formalities of spiritual direction as well. Conversations with faculty or friends at the Wharf, a small bar on campus (in the late 1970s), provided opportunities to talk more about a lecture or just to relax while having a beer.

I especially enjoyed following up with faculty on ideas that enlivened me—the concept of liminal experiences, for example, which we discussed in a class on liturgy. I had never heard of the concept, but once presented to me—and reinforced over beer, I realized how ubiquitous such experiences could be.

Everyone goes through liminal experiences—initiations, passages through one state of being to another (childhood to adolescence, adolescence to adulthood) as one passes through the threshold of a door, different realities, different beings, on either side, like "passages" in a book that take you from one place or character to another. The concept provided a structural foundation for much of my future thinking. I had not known anything like it before. I came to see the crossing of the bridge to St. Ben as itself a liminal experience, passing onto the irenic grounds so different from what seemed the aimless bustle beyond.

In the same way that I am formed (though less intentionally) by family and society at large, seminary formation carried with it an introduction to the culture of seminary life: gossip, a lack of charity, coarseness. Cut-downs of classmates, off-color jokes and camp, and constant murmuring about others served as a counterweight to the periods of insight I experienced. Or maybe they bolstered it—as though I could try out a new identity fraught with insecurity by lashing out with "superior" insights into others' weaknesses.

As Flannery O'Conner suggests to Betty Hester, seminarians are not the "saintly" people of stereotypes, but neither are they entirely sinners. Like you, like most people, seminarians are between, and one of the great benefits of formation is a growing consciousness (and eventual acceptance) of my and other people's mixed natures. Most of us are both saints and sinners, although society sometimes tries to peg us to one pole or the other.

Some of my confreres (and some students I taught later) acted as though they had it all figured out, thus short-circuiting the formation process by their certainty. Nevertheless, their exaggerated piety and resistance to intellectual work hinted more at fear than certitude. I cannot discount their experience because I also covered fear with bravado. We danced a dance between masking and unmasking.

What eventually became apparent to me was that formation opened in me not a sentimental piety, which tends to prioritize legalism and the trappings of religion, but the beginnings of a sober view of the church and oneself grounded in prayer and study.

Looking in the mirror and seeing your foibles, shortcomings, and pettiness, and then living with them is not easy task. Nor is it easy to accept those of others. Formation sometimes leads to a church that exaggerates the place of law and doctrine at the expense of the person. Nevertheless, the struggle for person—more than the apparent certainties of law—epitomizes seminary formation. And doctrine (law) doesn't appear so "certain" once you start studying it.

To say that I came to see myself and the world differently is true. But it's also true that I gained such a view through deep periods of doubt, through periods of hubris, and of seeing the speck in my brothers' eyes while missing the plank in my own. It's not a pleasant revelation, but as O'Connor says elsewhere, simply because you can't stomach the truth doesn't make it less true.

Even now, I can't say that I know myself well. What I can say is that I see more readily the mystery of the world and my (in between, shaky) place in it, wracked as the world is with the exaggerations and shortcomings of the humans who inhabit it, many eager to trade a sense of being between for the solid ground of certainty and the boundaries such certainty fosters. This stereotype may have been what Pound played on in his dismissal of Eliot's turn toward "Moses" and the church—not the openness that being between proffers, but a closure into what Pound presumably saw as religious legalism. However, I think that Eliot, like Gabriel Marcel, found mystery. Marcel suggests that problems have solutions, but mysteries should be experienced. Life isn't a problem but a mystery in which we participate. It's a hard-won perspective gained more than forty years after having graduated from St. Ben, and a view I often fail to maintain.

───

The Benedictine Monks at the Abbey have a strong tradition of liturgy, and daily Mass opened me to its simple rhythms—song, word, ritual action. I was not always good at getting up for morning prayer, but I usually made it to evening prayer. Evening prayer closed with the Canticle of Simeon, which became one of my favorites, a prayer I recited nightly with our kids many years later:

> At last oh powerful Master
> you give leave to your servant to go
> in peace according to your promise.
> For my eyes have seen your salvation
> which you have prepared for the nations
> a light to enlighten the gentiles
> and give glory to your people Israel.

> Give praise to the Father almighty,
> to his Son, Jesus Christ, the Lord,
> to the Spirit who dwells in our hearts,
> now and forever. Amen

My eyes did not always see the salvation of which Simeon speaks, but I became more confident of its presence, available for seeing. Such vision emerged, despite (and because of) feelings of instability, between a past I was coming to see as both formative and somewhat illusory and toward a future whose terminus was unclear.

While at St. Ben as both a student and later as faculty, I enjoyed not only the understated and powerful daily Masses, but I had the opportunity to witness several rites of monastic profession. The liturgy as a whole is beautiful, with the movement of the initiate into the arms, quite literally, of the community, when at the end, the newly professed monk greets each member of the community with a sign of peace.

Before the candidate prostrates himself in the sanctuary, he chants three times, arms outstretched in the open surrender of prayer, the following verse from Psalm 119: "Accept me, O Lord, as you have promised, that I may live, and let me not be put to shame in my hope."

I felt deeply moved.

When prostrated, a funeral pall is placed over him, and the litany of the saints is chanted. At the end of the litany, the funeral pall is removed slowly while the choir sings "Awake and live, Oh you who sleep; awake and rise from the dead. Let the light of Christ shine on you!" The candidate rises, having gone through a threshold, a liminal passage, and into life as a new person.

The ritual surrender, the plea for sustenance and protection, the symbolic death and resurrection made sense to me and stirred in me something that had begun at LSU. I longed for more of whatever it was.

Eventually, I came to see that what I longed for was longing itself. C.S. Lewis names this longing *sehnsucht*, "the inconsolable longing in the heart for we know not what...that unnamable something, desire for which pierces us like a rapier at the smell of a bonfire, the sound of wild ducks flying overhead" (*Pilgrim's Regress*). It is the sort of longing that made me happy and sad simultaneously. Intellectual formation at St. Ben taught me much about the names of things (such as liminal experiences) as well as the longing for an "unnamable something." I swam in the river of longing.

The tumult, the unbalance, the inversions and undulations of the time marked me deeply. What I had thought valuable I came to see as illusions of power and money, whose incessant attraction would afflict me later in life. Although the path I tread was meant to lead to ordained ministry, the end became less important than the discoveries, joys, and pitfalls along the way.

I tried to convey this joy of a discovery once in a conversation with my mother, who asked "What will you do with your degree if you don't become a priest?" I didn't know, but what I began to see about myself and the world was proving different from what I had understood it to be earlier.

For the first time, for example, I came to see the tenets of the church as something that could be explored intellectually as well as experienced (or waited for) daily. Introductory studies in Scripture and liturgy recast simplistic "how-does-this-make-you-feel" approaches that were prevalent in parish catechesis the late 1970s and early '80s. Pairing those studies with readings of Plato and Aristotle, Immanuel Kant, Carl Rogers, B.F. Skinner, Sigmund Freud, and others, created in me a sort of pinball effect. I bounced from view to view, hoping at some point I'd land on one that suited me.

In my studies at LSU, I had not imagined that the world or I could contain such varied contours. I found it hard to let go of assumptions about myself and my place in the world, but neither could I remain ignorant to the world opening before me. Formation ripped me apart only to pull me back together (provisionally) as time went on.

5

Both the believer and the unbeliever share, each in his own way, doubt *and* belief.
 −Joseph Ratzinger (Pope Benedict XVI),
 Introduction to Christianity

I graduated from St. Ben in May of 1980, went to Europe that summer with a classmate (who much later became the abbot of St. Ben), and enrolled in Notre Dame Seminary in New Orleans in the fall.

If you begin priestly formation in college, you attend a "minor" (college) seminary, like St. Ben, which lays the foundations of philosophical and theological studies in preparation for formation and studies at a "major" (graduate-level) seminary. Notre Dame in New Orleans is a major seminary.

Like St. Ben, Notre Dame educates seminarians from the region. Students come from dioceses in Mississippi, Alabama, and Florida, as well as Louisiana and Texas. Some of the young monks at Saint Joseph Abbey also begin their studies for priesthood there. Notre Dame leads men more deeply into their priestly formation while offering studies in the major branches of theology—ecclesiology, Scripture, church history, moral theology, pastoral theology, spiritual theology, speculative theology, doctrine, canon law. As a first-year student, I took introductory courses in most of those areas, except canon law.

The faculty consisted of a variety of priests and a few lay persons: Jesuits, Dominicans, Marists, diocesan priests from New Orleans and "on loan" from other dioceses. Outstanding among them was John Carville, a priest of the diocese of Baton Rouge and the lesser-known cousin of James Carville, the outspoken democratic consultant and political guru. John taught moral theology—at the time we read Bernard Haring, among others—and he was as soft spoken and thoughtful as his cousin is loud. I remember him telling us a story about his time in Rome. He happened to walk into the Gesú (the main Jesuit Church) one day to be swallowed by beautiful organ music. When the music stopped, he went up to organ loft to tell the organist how much he enjoyed the impromptu recital—only to discover the organist was Albert Schweitzer!

Father Carville required short papers on assigned readings, which forced me to grapple with the material while honing my writing. I didn't save the papers from his class (though I wish I had). I recall one I wrote using a "Point/Counterpoint" format—imitating the popular segment of CBS's "Sixty Minutes," featuring James Kirkpatrick representing the conservative viewpoint and Shana Alexander offering the liberal one. The segment was famously lampooned in the early days of Saturday Night Live, with the "conservative" Dan Ackroyd saying to the "liberal" Jane Curtain: "Jane, you ignorant slut!" In the early 1980s it was an oft-quoted line. I didn't use that line, but a variation of it, which I can't recall now. In any case, Father Carville loved the piece and read it to the class.

I mention this not just because I was happy that the piece was well-received, but because it became the first of many pieces I wrote as spoofs on popular programs. When I was Dean at St. Ben, I wrote "The News from Saint Benedict"—an obvious take on Garrison Keillor's "The News from Lake Woebegone." When I was director of communications, I wrote, "The Abbey Scream," a lampoon of "The Abbey Voice," which I wrote and edited. These forays into the comic and mildly transgressive gave me a creative outlet and bolstered a sense of confidence in my writing.

In a class on church history, we read Justo Gonalez's first two volumes of his *A History of the Catholic Church*. The Christological controversies of the early church fascinated me—the serious debates that struggled with the nature of the person of Jesus. Was his humanity only an appearance that veiled his divine nature, as the Docetists would have it? Was he an emanation of a lesser demi-urge, as the Gnostics might have it? Was he simply a human on whom God bestowed special gifts, as the Arians would say? In short, how could he be fully divine and fully human at the same time? The struggles of the early church suggested to me that church doctrine was not something "etched in stone," law forever unchanging, but part of an historical development and settled only after several centuries of debate—about the *person* of Jesus.

One of the faculty had encouraged me to petition the Archbishop to attend the North American College in Rome. The Archdiocese of New Orleans had not sent a seminarian there for many years, and they were not inclined to do so. They wanted to support their own seminary. My trip to Europe, with an extended visit to Rome and the Italian countryside, had opened a new vista of possibilities for study. Certainly, I wanted the "honor" of being chosen to go there, but I also wanted to live in Rome!

My year at Notre Dame became a year of wanting to move beyond Notre Dame. I engaged with the program but also grew impatient with it. I engaged with classmates but didn't develop lasting friendships among them—as I did at St. Ben. My longest lasting friendships were with the young monks from St. Ben who studied there. Despite my impatience with parts of the program at Notre Dame, I can attribute a central part of my growing spirituality to a class on spiritual theology offered by Fr. Clarence Menard.

Fr. Menard was a friend of Fr. Roy's, who had suggested I get to know him. Fr. Roy said he was "deeply spiritual" and a good teacher, both true. I didn't get to know him well, but in his class, I first read *The Way of a Pilgrim*, about the pilgrim's quest for "unceasing prayer" St. Paul calls for in his letter to the community at Thessaloniki.

Something clicked in me when I read the book. I don't know exactly what, perhaps the romantic in me was drawn to the pilgrim's simplicity and poverty, wandering from town to town (a foreshadowing of my many moves years later?), and his quest. Up to this point I had not given much thought to St. Paul urging the Thessalonians to "pray unceasingly." But the pilgrim's solution, to pray the Jesus Prayer, seemed right. The prayer, "Lord Jesus Christ, have mercy on me, a sinner" offers itself to the rhythm of breath or of walking, and its plea, acknowledging a fundamental need of mercy, touched a sense of unworthiness I felt which was paradoxically accompanied by a sense of well-being offered. Was it an unconscious recognition of my "in-between place," of my doubt, my hubris at wanting to leave Notre Dame to pursue studies in Rome? I don't know, but the Jesus Prayer has been part of my life since that time.

The archbishop gave me the OK to study abroad in spring of 1981. I filled out the documentation, was accepted, and began working on the myriad details of a move to the North American College. I took a class in Italian at the New Orleans World Trade Center. My mother sewed my laundry number (132?) into each item of my clothing, since our laundry was done for us by sisters at the College. This in 1981!

Much later, when I was in graduate school at LSU, James Olney gave me a tape of poems I'd listen to on my commute to and from LSU. On it, Richard Wilbur reads his "Love Calls Us to the Things of This World." In the poem, he describes the "difficult balance" of nuns doing laundry, and he calls for there to be only laundry on earth. I always thought of those sisters, whom I rarely saw, when I listened to Wilbur's poem, somewhere on Interstate 12 between Covington and Baton Rouge.

Many religious sisters I know would not look kindly on his quasi-romantic vision of laundry and sisters. Sometimes I had pangs of guilt as I listened, thinking about the sisters whose lives centered on washing my clothes and the clothes of future priests. No wonder a culture of clericalism persists! I thought of Wilbur as just another stodgy Catholic who didn't mind keeping women in their place.

And yet, Wilbur's poem wrestles with more than that, and as I listened to it time and again, it took on different hues. It became, in its way, Christological, opening an incarnational view of simple things like washing clothes, and the inherent imbalance between love of the things of the world and love of God—or better, of finding love of God through the things of the world, a sacramental vision.

Still, I never complained about the sisters doing my laundry. And I'm getting rather ahead of my story.

Back to New Orleans! I happily made preparations for my departure.

Fr. Roy could barely contain his enthusiasm. He spoke about me at Masses, bragged to fellow priests about me, and insisted that the parish hold a "send-off" liturgy for me. The parish liturgy committee made special felt banners (common in the early 1980s)—one that read "Given in Service," another that said "Led by the Spirit." Hanging at the front of the altar, yet another banner displayed a silhouette of a person (me) inside the threshold of an opened door (a liminal passage!), a white path leading to a silhouette of St. Peter's Basilica, with "Bon Voyage! Arrivederci! Vale!" spread across the top, my name next to the door, and at the bottom, "May Your Heart Be Always Open."

The vocation director, Bobby Muench, a future bishop, offered a final blessing over me, the parish extending their hands as well as Fr. Roy, my mother and father, and a young priest from Detroit, Mike Nardone, who for a time served as our parish choir director, a family friend who came back for the service.

Blessing at farewell Mass. New Orleans, LA, 1982. Fr Roy (with glasses), Robert Muench, and Mike Nardone, with my parents behind me.

Banner at farewell Mass. Note its "liminal" character.

Jerrie and Debbie, with their husbands and young families came to New Orleans for the Mass, as did my mother's cousin, Sr. Jane, one of the Marianite Sisters with whom my mother had always been close.

I was embarrassed and honored at the same time. It surprises me that, given the array of memories I recall as I now write, I don't remember anything about the content of the "mini-homily" Fr. Roy asked me to give at the end of Mass, though I found a copy of it after writing this. The send-off was, perhaps, too much "about me" although an accurate measure of the pride Fr. Roy felt at having "one of his own" so chosen.

Sometime in July of 1981, I arrived at Fiumicino and was met by Deacon Ed, a third-year student from the diocese of Denver. Ed represented but one of the many dioceses who sent students to the College. Though he was from the west, I would learn that the majority of students came from dioceses on the East Coast, particularly New England.

Ed gave me an impromptu tour as we drove into the city, weaving in and out of the Fiats and Vespas and Alfa Romeos, speeding and passing on small city streets like an Italian. He enjoyed my worried look and white knuckles. When Bramante's dome of St. Peter's came into view, my nerves settled into excitement, and if I had displayed any signs of jet lag, they disappeared.

We climbed the Janiculum Hill (*il Gianicolo*), Ed honked the horn at the gate, and the *portiere* opened it. Here I was! I had arrived at the famous North American College.

I don't remember the first few days at NAC (as the college was familiarly known). I do remember the aura of the place—a place where many US bishops had gone to study, a storied place, full of tradition.

My room was on the second floor (what would be the equivalent of the third floor in the US because the ground floor isn't termed the first floor). Like any residence hall, the room was simple: a single bed, a desk, a small closet, but unlike other dorm rooms, this one had a window that looked out through the umbrella pines toward St. Peter's Basilica and its famous dome. A heavy wooden shutter with a pulley mechanism (I had never seen these before) blocked the midday sun and softened the perennial Roman noise. The "New Men" (the name for first-year students) were given tours of the building. We needed to locate the dining hall (wine was served at lunch!), the chapel, the mail room, for example. Writing out the address *Collegio*

Americano del Nord, Citta del Vaticano 00120, on my shipping crate in the US had seemed magical to me. I was here!

We toured outside as well, a large field surrounded by a paved path for running, or as I later discovered, for the famous Italian tradition of the *passegiato*, handball courts, and the separate nuns' residence.

One of the first group outings was to the Questura to get a required student visa. Given the reputation of the Italian bureaucracy, the New Men were told to prepare themselves for a long wait. Fortunately, an upperclassman who spoke Italian fluently handled the paperwork. We needed simply to be "present" so as to confirm our corporeal entry into the country and our residence at NAC. I had been reading Camus's *The Plague*, so I had it with me. I found myself somewhat nervous about being with the other New Men and wanted a book to shield my shaky self.

The New Men took an introductory Italian language class. Much of it was a rehash of the class I had taken in New Orleans. A small, spinsterish-looking Italian woman led the class. She reinforced what I had covered in New Orleans and introduced me further to the grammar and pronunciation of *la lingua piu bella del mondo*. We also had meetings with NAC's staff, which included Fr. Laurence Bronkiewicz, the Academic Dean. Larry became my spiritual director, a good friend, and eventually godfather to all of Jan's and my children. We called him "Uncle Larry."

New Men performed an annual talent show not long after their arrival. A former English barrister performed one of Hamlet's soliloquies. I told him I was impressed with it. A brilliant, sometimes acerbic, student from Iowa, said, "For some reason people always think Shakespeare sounds better if recited with a British accent." I remember thinking he was right, though I had not thought of it until he said it. I ended up playing a medley of guitar pieces (the Beatles, John Denver) with a fellow from the Archdiocese of Boston.

After orientation and language training, but before the first semester of classes began, New Men were encouraged to take a trip away from Rome. I chose to travel to the Amalfi Coast, where I stayed at the Pensione Puppetto, and took the train out of Stazioni Termini to the South.

I didn't know what to expect, but I didn't expect such beauty—the deep blue and clear waters of the Mediterranean Sea, the sumptuous food, the hospitality of the Italians! Several other New Men had decided on the same place, so we ended up with about ten or so NACers there. I oiled my skin (no sunscreen in the early 1980s) sat out on the rocky beach to tan, drank wine, and ate calamari for the first time.

I wanted to get around the cove, so I looked up the word for "renting," hoping to take one of the pensione's kayaks out on the water. When I tried my broken Italian, "*Io vorrei noleggiare un kayak*," the patient manager told me something in his rapid Italian that I didn't quite understand. But I did hear the word "*libra*" and came to understand I could take it out for free. What a wonderful place!

And yet, while in Positano, we got the news that Anwar Sadat had been assassinated. Although I understood little of the historical complexities that led to this horrific act, I sat on the beach that night to wonder when the "Holy Land" would see an end to senseless murders.

Back in Rome, I grew accustomed to the walk from NAC to the Greg, which was about two miles and took about twenty minutes each way. Most days, I walked with a group of second year students who took me under their wing. We followed various routes, some defined by food—*gelato* or *pizza rustica*—or some by landmarks or streets—Piazza Navona and the Pantheon, Via del Corso, Via Giulia, Campo dei Fiori, Fontana di Trevi. The routes themselves formed a branch of the traditions generations of students relived at NAC. Our de facto leader, Brian, from Long Island, often chose the route for us: "How about Piazza Navona today?" We usually walked in groups of four or five, talking about classes, cutting up or gossiping with quick-witted banter or solid concern during tough times, which came around often enough.

I sought the humor of the life while also appreciating its gravity, sought the pleasure of being in the cradle of the church, while also trying not to take myself too seriously. I often failed, but became somewhat more used to my failures. Some folks called NAC and Rome a "hell-hole." I didn't see it that way, but reveled in its aura of romance and culture and tradition, even if I sometimes felt ill-suited to the life.

I remember walking through Piazza Navona at Christmas time—every imaginable type of *presepio* available for purchase. I remember the souvenir shops next to the Vatican, a three-dimensional blond-haired, blue-eyed Jesus, arms extended on the cross, face bloodied by his crown of thorns, winked at me as I walked by, as though we were in on a cosmic joke. I found the shops garish but inevitable. Everyone needs to make a buck—or several *lire*. These shop owners were not the only ones to capitalize on gaudy piety.

I remember dinners with Larry at Vecchio Roma or Cecilia Matella. He introduced me to Fontana Candida and Negronis, along with spaghetti alle vongole, penne arrabiata, and pasta carbonara.

A priest of the Diocese of Bridgeport, Connecticut, Larry represented to me an image of the cultured New Englander, even though, as I came to find out, his parents were part of the post-War immigrant middle class. The son of a Polish-American father (who died when Larry was very young) and a French mother, Larry spoke French at home and was fluent in Italian because he had studied in Rome many years—not only at NAC, but also at the graduate house—Casa Santa Maria (near the Gregorian University)—where he pursued a doctorate in spirituality. His dissertation was titled "The Spiritual Impulse of Ronald Knox." I knew nothing about Knox at the time, but Larry's study of him added to my image of him as a refined New Englander.

Soft spoken, somewhat droll—he loved his own jokes, often breaking out in sardonic laughter after his punch line—he nevertheless had a reputation among NACers for being funereal. His nickname was "Chiller." One would-be comic among the students joked at a school-wide evening of entertainment that Larry could not see because of the "pennies on his eyes." The auditorium erupted in laughter, but I didn't get the joke. Larry told me later that the fellow was suggesting he was so "low-key" that he was dead, and the pennies referred to the old funerary practice of placing coins on the eyes of the dead to keep them shut. He was not happy about the joke. "Just because I'm reticent," he said, "doesn't mean that I don't experience things deeply." I respected him for opening up to me, though once he explained the joke, I laughed too!

In any event, Larry was a good listener, even when my mother assailed him about birth control many years later. I found it easy to talk with him about life at NAC, to joke with him about Roman inefficiency, and about family. As an only child, he found my large family fascinating, and prodded me to talk about them. I found myself babbling about them, and also about Fr. Roy, about my attraction to the spirit of the 1960s, challenging the "status quo," a la Bob Dylan, rebelling against spoken and unspoken dogma in search of an "authentic" life in "times that were a'changing."

I remember once saying to him that "I may have been born a decade late," because I saw the changes in the church brought about by Vatican II consonant with the cultural upheavals of that decade. In the early 1980s, a backlash to that spirit had already begun with what I saw as the rigidities of John Paul II's papacy, including a mandate that seminarians beyond a certain point in their formation wear clerical garb when out on the streets of Rome. I followed the mandate, though I didn't like it. Among my babblings, Larry picked up on implicit and explicit references to my growing ambivalence toward what I saw as the strictures of priestly life.

I loved Rome, loved being away from the United States, what I saw as suburban aridity, and loved being in a city brimming with history and culture. I remember walking to Pizzaria IVO in Trastevere, cobbled streets half lit, stuccoed buildings glowing, lovers holding hands or kissing in the soft light. I remember the steamed windows of the Fiats or Citroens that bounced rhythmically with the sex of their occupants. Walking down the Gianiculum hill toward NAC we often found used condoms in a park near the office of the Propagation of the Faith, which was on the way. We laughed and called the park "Propagation Park." For me, the laughter masked a longing to know such pleasure.

I remember walking down via Giulia during a music festival, muted lights leading straight down to the Palazzo Farnese. A melancholy, reflective though happy, mood enveloped me as I walked from villa to villa, in which I listened to the sad strains of a cello or violin, a mournful solo piano, or string quartets. At one performance, I felt overcome by Lewis' *sehnsucht*, the world opening to me in splendor even as it eluded me and left me wanting more. Even here, now, as I recollect this memory, I see the dimly lit street and feel a tug of longing.

I don't possess a great knowledge of classical music. I listen to it, but can't identify it easily or speak intelligibly about it. But I experience certain pieces deeply. So I see my experience on Via Giulia that night as a precursor to my neck prickling whenever I listen to Beethoven's Ninth, especially the "Ode to Joy," and to a deep sense of mournful longing I felt listening to the "Saturday Night Waltz" movement of Copland's *Rodeo* as I once drove the Causeway between New Orleans and Mandeville alone late one night. Those pieces continue to move me, especially Copland's melancholy bassoon rising and falling quietly—in the background, as right and involuntary as breathing.

Rome enchants both above the ground and below it. When I went to the catacombs of Santa Priscilla for the first time, I felt swept into a romantic current of early Christianity. Later when my mother and a friend visited, and a priest-friend from Louvain celebrated Mass in the catacombs for us, I felt the presence of early Christians, huddled, afraid, yet happy—like me—for the explosion of something new that had burst upon them. That feeling expanded when I first visited San Clemente, near the famous Colosseum, and walked through its layered history—down into the darkness of a second-century mithraeum, climbing up into a fourth-century basilica, and then up to a tenth-century basilica at street level. Life above and below.

In Rome, history, like memory, abounds, and sometimes it's easily retrieved. More often than not, however, it takes years of patient excavation and scholarship—like digging through memory in words, as I do now.

I remember that Jean Vanier, the founder of L'Arche, a group of Christians dedicated to the service of the physically or mentally challenged, gave a talk at NAC about his work (long before scandal shook the movement). His work with the forgotten and marginalized seemed to me an image of Jesus among the lepers. Vanier appeared to embody a selfless life, and in thinking so, I, like millions of others, was duped by his seeming grace. Is it possible that some good has come from L'Arche despite the founder's deep iniquity? In my memory, Vanier's talk finds juxtaposition with an impromptu lecture from Fr. Bryan Heir, someone about whom I knew nothing, but whose scholarship flowed effortlessly in paragraphs, without notes. I hoped someday to emulate his eloquence and clarity. I enjoyed the down-to-earth brilliance of Reggie Foster, the "Pope's Latinist," wearing his workman's clothes as he led our class of stuffy seminarians in a Latin rendition of "Three Blind Mice."

Life above and below, sacred and profane, conscious and unconscious. All these meshed easily in Rome—and thus opened beautiful interstitial spaces, between the poles of the dualities. At that time, I thought I needed to keep the poles separate. Here, now, I see more beauty in their tremulous tension.

My mother and a friend visited in spring of 1982. Larry got them a room at a hotel near the 1960 Olympic grounds. We ate breakfast there, then played tourist in and around the city. Although I loved the travel, I must have appeared standoffish or aloof to my mother, who worried that I was not enjoying myself. She noted that a DaVinci exhibition in Florence seemed to be the only thing I enjoyed. I don't recall precisely what bothered me, if anything. More than likely my mood reflected my growing misgivings of the life I was following.

I had begun to consider my departure from the seminary, although I kept my considerations to myself. The thought of leaving frightened me. I didn't want to disappoint Fr. Roy, Larry, new friends at NAC, or my parents, nor did I have a plan about what I'd do if I left. And because I found in Rome and Italy a great openness, and though I was happy to see my mother, her presence may have taken me back to a more constricted place. In Rome and at NAC, I had begun to establish an identity apart from Louisiana, home, and family. All of those rushed back with her visit, though I don't think I was aware of it at the time. These unconscious feelings likely manifested themselves in an attitude of world weariness or boredom, and of taking myself too seriously. So, I probably did seem "off" to her. Certainly, it was another instance of being off-balance—being between.

⤴

The summer after my mother's visit, I worked as a Chaplain's Assistant at Bitburg Air Base in Germany. Part of the formation program required that seminarians engage in a period of extended pastoral work. I don't recall if I chose this assignment or if was chosen for me, but I looked forward to being in Germany again—a place I had visited on my European tour after graduating from St. Ben.

While at the base, I remember visiting the house of a young married woman—one of the pilot's wives?— who asked, "Do you like being a seminarian?" It was a question I got often. I responded as I usually did, "I really like living in Rome and being with folks from all over the United States, but," I continued, "I sometimes find the life difficult."

She said, somewhat out of context, "You are very handsome, you know." Well, I guess I knew, and I was flattered but slightly embarrassed at her saying so. Fr. Roy had told me a cautionary tale before I left New Orleans. He said I might find myself in a situation in which a woman might tell me that I could "leave my shoes under her bed," a phrase I had not heard before but whose meaning seemed clear enough. I don't know if this situation represented such a case or if this woman only wanted to offer support—most likely the latter. In any case, I thanked her politely, changed the subject, and soon left.

The Catholic chaplain, a Major under whom I worked in Bitburg, had been posted around the world, most recently in Japan. Out of shape, a cigarette always in his smoked-stained fingers, he worried whether he could pass the Air Force physical, which required, among other things, that he complete a mile, walking or jogging, in less than ten minutes. He failed. He had a smarminess I didn't like, and though I stayed for a while in his apartment, I tried to avoid him as much as possible. My internal radar told me something was amiss. One night, not entirely to my dismay, my misgivings were confirmed.

I walked into a completely dark apartment—save for the glow of a cigarette across the room. When I turned on the light, I saw Fr. Major in a Japanese robe, apparently with nothing underneath. He tried to engage in small talk, but I walked directly to my room quickly after the mildest of pleasantries. Luckily, the other priest assigned to the base soon left for vacation, and I was able to stay at his place for the remainder of my time. Was Fr. Major coming on to me? Did he think he could? Had I given him any indication that I was interested? I didn't think so, nor can I say even now what his intentions might have been. I can say, however, that his greeting and his attire alarmed me.

At the end of the program I received a glowing evaluation from the Major (a cover for his possible indiscretion?) and from the Colonel who headed the Chaplaincy program, a man I admired but didn't know well and whom I hadn't even realized would offer an evaluation of my work.

In Bitburg, a young married couple came to see me because they found their relationship in turmoil. I was almost twenty-three years old, and they were my age or just younger. The young man didn't want to be there. He fidgeted, gave me sidelong glances, and grew more and more impatient as I offered one platitude about relationships after another. Horribly ill-prepared to deal with whatever problems they faced, I offered what I could, but mostly stammered, caught up in my own unease about confronting a "real-life" issue while growing more aware of my own "issues," especially those surrounding sexuality and the prospect of celibacy. I had thought married life might be better than the celibate life of a priest, but this couple reminded me that both have their challenges.

In any case, the conversation came around to music, which interested the husband. I loaned him my guitar in the hope his connection to music might help in reconnecting (I didn't know how) to the relationship with his wife. I don't know what happened to the couple or whether the guitar helped or not. I had to ask him several times to return it, and after he did, I never saw or heard from them again. I hardly felt I had "succeeded" in helping them.

⁓

Years later, when I taught Graham Green's *Monsignor Quixote* in classes on Catholic writers, I often thought of this young married couple when the eponymous Monsignor complained: "Why do I never find the right words?" I think of it again as I now write, as I search for the right words to re-member and re-collect the passages of my life.

⁓

The Lutheran chaplain at the base had an office lined with books on theology, spirituality, and—surprise—sexuality. I often lingered there, pulling interesting titles between small administrative tasks or while waiting for appointments. The eclectic nature of his collection displayed an unexpected broadness. A book on sexual pleasure for married couples! Books on the spirituality of nature! And the sermons of Paul Tillich, some of whose work—*The Courage to Be*—I had read at St. Ben and later at Notre Dame. The chaplain also kept a binder of his typed sermons. I read those with delight and some awe. Here was an integrated man, I thought, theology, spirituality, and sexuality finding an easy home with one another—and without what I saw as the "problem" of celibacy, increasingly the focus of my struggles.

While at Notre Dame in New Orleans, I befriended a Franciscan priest who saw celibacy as a real gift, one that opened him to satisfying and deep friendships with men and women without a concomitant desire for carnal consumption. Not all priests and seminarians, including myself, could call themselves so blessed (or lucky).

During the time of my formation, the guidance for seminarians on celibacy included, among other things, the idea of "sublimation" of sexual urges—not to deny the energy, but to channel it into other productive activity. Celibacy permitted the freedom, so the thinking went, for multiple and communal relationships instead of a particular one, which might impede the role of a pastor in a parish. This ideology worked for my Franciscan friend, but I found celibacy less a gift and more a burden. I remember telling my Franciscan friend that instead of freeing me, celibacy produced in me excessive thoughts of what I couldn't have, sort of like St. Paul saying that the law leads to sin:

> The law entered in so that transgression might increase but, where sin increased, grace overflowed all the more. . . . What then shall we say? Shall we persist in sin that grace may abound? Of course not! How can we who died to sin yet live in it? (Romans 5:20–21, 6)

I understand this passage to say that without the law, sin would not be possible, and thus grace may not have been offered. Paul sees that he is awfully close to saying that grace is "caused" by sin ("Shall we persist in sin that grace may abound?") so he proclaims that by baptism ("death to sin") grace is freely given. I realize I'm stretching the analogy, but I saw celibacy not as part of a redemptive grace freely given, but as "law" that increased my sin—"transgressive" thoughts about what I knew I would not have.

※

During the latter part of the fall 1982 semester, I had to decide whether to petition (or not) for ordination to the diaconate in the spring of '83. I made the petition to do so, announced my decision to family and friends, some of whom made plans to attend the ordination in April, but I found myself bothered by a lingering sense of doubt.

By this time, Larry and I were good friends. He knew me well, understood my joys and my preoccupations. Sometime in late December as we talked about the diaconate, he said, "You know, I see that you like very much the intellectual challenges of theology."

"Yes, I do," I said, feeling somewhat proud.

"But," he continued, "I don't see in you a strong desire for the priestly life."

His words hit me hard. I felt unmasked and begrudgingly admitted that he was right. "Yes, I really enjoy philosophy and theology," I said, "but you may be right. I can't always envision myself as a priest. I just don't know, though."

He suggested that I give myself some time, a couple of weeks or so, to pray and to think things over.

I took long walks around the Villa Borghese and the Piazza del Popolo, down the via Babouini to Piazza di Spagna. I walked along the Lungo Tevere, through Trastevere, and further up the Gianicolo. I even took a train out to the beach to pray among the dunes—mostly empty during the winter months.

I can't remember everything I thought of or prayed about during these walks. I'm sure I berated myself for being indecisive, wondered what Fr. Roy and the vocation director, Bobby Muench (who had led the final blessing at my going-away Mass) would say, worried about my parents' reaction. Was I being selfish? Was I denying a call to priestly life? Had there even been a call in the first place? Why couldn't I see things more clearly? Would I ever find direction in my life?

I don't know if I carried on a dialogue with myself, but if I did, I think I would remember it, so momentous a time it was. But maybe its very momentousness shields it from retrieval now. I probably had an ongoing internal dialogue for months, and it may have gone something like this:

What do you want to do?
I don't know! I've been in the seminary more than five years, and I still can't say.
Well?
Well what?
What's wrong with you?
Maybe nothing! Maybe this wasn't what I was supposed to do anyway. Maybe I've deluded myself and others all along.
How do you know?
I don't!
Do you think you can help people in their struggles?
Yes and no.
Can you do this outside of the priesthood?
Maybe, but Fr. Roy told me once that he is a priest because it's the only thing that makes sense for him.

Is priesthood the only thing that makes sense for you?
Not really.
What else makes sense?
I don't know, a lot of things—marriage, travel, reading, writing.
Do you want to be celibate?
Not really.
Do you want to live in a rectory by yourself or with another priest?
Not really.
What will you do if you leave?
I don't know!
Why did you pursue the seminary in the first place?
Well, I thought I could help people and I wanted to please people, especially Fr. Roy and Mom and Dad. Neither did I mind all the attention it brought me. And I thought maybe, just maybe, God was suggesting that I do it.
Will you try to please people all your life?
I hope not! But it's something that comes "naturally" to me. And it seems better than displeasing them.
What does God want you to do?
I don't know. I guess he wants me to be happy.
Can you be happy as a priest?
Maybe, though probably not. I think I would get lonely and want to be married.
So?
Maybe you're right; I shouldn't stick myself into a life thinking it will be lonely, with a desire always to want something I cannot have.

And this, perhaps, is how I admitted to myself that I didn't want the priestly life—the parish councils, the "everyday" tasks, the lonely celibate life in a rectory, always thinking that I was missing out on something I thought I wanted more.

I liked theology and philosophy, liked the camaraderie of my life at NAC, but couldn't envision myself as a priest. I felt relieved!

I called my parents, who, despite my fear, supported my decision. I called Bobby Muench, the vocation director in New Orleans, who said he was sorry to hear it but he understood. I called Fr. Roy, who said much the same thing, but in whose voice I detected a shade of sorrow.

About that same time, I heard from Chris, who lived next door to me at LSU when I was a freshman in college. He called me in Rome to tell me that he was entering the Jesuits, that he had thought about my discernment to enter the seminary more than five years ago. Feeling a bit sheepish, I congratulated him, but told him I had decided to leave the seminary. I don't remember his reaction to my news, but we have followed each other's lives closely since that call. He lived at the Jesuit house near the apartment I eventually rented in New Orleans, so we saw each other from time to time. He finished philosophy at Loyola University and then went to Yale to study Christian Ethics.

Fun-loving, serious, rather obsessive-compulsive—a trait he attributes to his studies in engineering and his family—Chris became a long-standing family friend. He walked me through fears of joining Jan back in Rome in 1985, and years later, when the kids were old enough to joke around, he entertained them by poking fun at my own obsessive-compulsive tendencies. He especially liked imitating a high-pitched voice I used whenever I tried to defend a defenseless statement. The kids loved our repartee, seeing their dad challenged and made fun of. Now, as adults, they enjoy making fun of me too.

Chris is now a professor of Christian Ethics at Georgetown University and editor of *Theological Studies*—still, if not more, obsessive-compulsive, still very funny, and still a good friend.

⁓

I could have stayed in Rome to finish the degree in the spring term, but I thought that my presence there would have been contradictory. Since the seminary was for men who were headed for priesthood, and since I had concluded priesthood was not for me, I decided to leave after the end of the fall term, which in the Roman University system, finished in late January.

I left on February 5, 1983, a date I remember easily because it is Larry's birthday. He and a few classmates met me downstairs at "Firmum Est," a foyer with the College's crest on the floor.

That cold February morning, I wore a corduroy jacket, jeans, and desert boots—the "civies" I had worn for years. A knowing kindness and support filled the foyer. My friends had doubts about their paths, so they understood and respected my decision. Despite their doubts, their belief stood firm, so the spirit of support carried with it a somber tone. I was their friend, and I was leaving.

What would become of me? Would their hearts remain steadfast, as the crest in the foyer, which read "*Firmum Est Cor Meum*," announced? Apparently, my heart held more doubt than steadfastness. At least doubt in the priestly life. They had made their decision as I had made mine, and though we both faced futures unknown, theirs held more shape.

Life above and below, sacred and profane, conscious and unconscious, belief and doubt.

On the return flight, I was in the middle of the middle row of five seats on a 747. I sat next to an academic, a fellow who had been in Rome for a conference at the World Food Program headquarters. We made small talk. I told him I had been a student in Rome but was heading home. He asked: "How did you find the women there?" I must have looked a bit surprised, but gathered myself to tell him I had been studying for the priesthood. He blanched and said he hoped he hadn't offended me. I told him he had not, but our conversation stalled after that—he, afraid he had transgressed a "sacred" line, and I, somewhat embarrassed for him yet also awkward that I had not had the experiences he wanted to discuss.

I watched the onboard film, *Singing in the Rain*, which I had never seen, and remember feeling caught up in its joy!

Suspended in the liminal space between the heavens and the Earth, and with the shakiness of light turbulence, I felt a world open and fresh.

6

O waste of lost, in the hot mazes, lost, among bright stars on this weary, unbright cinder, lost! Remembering speechlessly we seek the great forgotten language, the lost lane-end into heaven, a stone, a leaf, an unfound door.

–Thomas Wolfe, *Look Homeward Angel*

I was met at the New Orleans airport by my mom and dad, and we returned to the house on Mimosa Court where I took up residence in my old bedroom. John was at Centenary College, and Mike, who married just before I left for Rome, was no longer in New Orleans. I would be alone at the house with my parents.

I recall the ride home from the airport, a strange feeling of the familiar and unfamiliar as we rode past the cemeteries in Metairie on our right and Mid-City on our left, the Superdome, and rising over the great Mississippi River on the bridge to the West Bank. The ride down General DeGaulle to our neighborhood, Tall Timbers, had changed little. I had changed, however, and looked out at the drabness—grass growing in the cracks of the side streets, run-down strip malls, and bland architecture. Had it always been so?

I took a trip to Denver to visit with my sister Polly, her husband, Jim, and their kids, Bret, David, and Stephanie. We skied, watched movies on Jim's laser disc player, and they invited friends over for a dinner party, one of whom was a priest they had come to know. After several glasses of wine and liqueurs, the priest and I took a walk in the brisk evening air.

Since the trip we took to see them in Canada in 1972, I had visited Polly and Jim several times. My first time on an airplane was in 1974, and it was a trip to see them when they lived in Calgary, where I learned to snow ski. When they moved to Denver, I went up to see them as well as to ski. Polly had become very active in her local parish, and that's how the priest ended up at this meal in 1983.

I don't remember his name, but I remember his encouragement. It's one of many times that people, sensing the difficulties of my about-face on the path toward priesthood, offered space. Fr. Roy had done it, though I felt he was disappointed. My friends among the monks at St. Joseph Abbey had done it, and now this fellow, whom I did not know, suggested that I take the time to find my way, no matter what that way might be.

In the distance that Denver offered and in the semi-haze of our wine-enhanced conversation, I welcomed not only the chance to clear my head in the cold evening air, but I also found solace. I didn't know where I was headed, but the lack of a plan was okay.

Despite the challenges of their life with three young children, Polly and Jim had cared enough to make space for me too.

I stayed with my parents for a couple of months, and while there, I developed unexpected friendships. Some young couples had moved onto the block with their young families. Ranging in age from three or four to eight or nine, the kids took delight in having a semi-adult willing to play football or chase or faux wrestling. They rang the doorbell to my parents' home to ask, "Can Eddie come out to play?" I enjoyed the wild energy of the kids, and their company allowed me respite from brooding over the overriding question of this time, *What was I going to do now?* I write this in a post-priest-scandal world, of course. In 1983, the scandals had not yet erupted. In today's world, I doubt parents would allow their kids to ring the doorbell and ask to play with a former seminarian.

<hr>

One of my older cousins and her husband had a house on Constantinople Street. Not long after my return from Rome, they planned a trip abroad and asked me to house-sit for them. I looked forward to house-sitting, especially on Constantinople. I had read *Confederacy of Dunces* while in Rome and wanted to reside for a time on the street made famous by Ignatius J. Reilly. They asked me to cut their very small lawn (with a hand mower—they didn't like gas mowers) and offered me the use of their car, a coppery orange Toyota Tercel.

I was still in touch with one of my former professors at Notre Dame who had undergone a rigorous weight-loss program. He had always been overweight, but he was very funny, quit-witted, and mischievous. The weight added to his Falstaffian character.

He had become enamored of his weight-loss therapist, the wife of a well-established physician. One night, he and I went out to eat and have a few drinks in the French Quarter. As we walked after dinner he told me that his therapist was attending a reception at one of the nearby hotels. We walked by to see if we might spot her. When he saw her, he asked if I would go in to ask her to come out to see him. I was not keen on the idea—I'm usually more reserved—but his mischievousness had not melted away with his excess weight, and I got caught up in it. The memory has a cinematographic quality to it.

There in the lobby, the therapist's husband sat in a plush chair holding forth among friends. In walks a stranger (me!), who speaks to the man's wife. She inclines her ear to the stranger's mouth to hear what he had to say: "Someone you know well is outside and would like to see you." The man looks up, asks what's going on, and the stranger says only that "someone" would like to see his wife. He looks to his wife, retains his dignified air, but the stranger notes the slightest of hurts around his eyes and mouth. The therapist and the stranger exit the lobby where my friend is waiting across the street. I stand off to allow my friend and the woman space for their furtive meeting. After a few moments, the women returns to the group inside. We walk away in the darkness among the tourists.

About a year and a half later, my friend left the priesthood.

Before he left, however, I took my cousin's car to visit him in Florida, where he stayed in a beach condominium his therapist owned. She was not there and she had no plans, as far as I know, to be there during his stay. We talked about her and about his weight loss. We talked about my uncertain future. I told him about a particularly scary night I had just the week before on Constantinople Street. Despite the spirit of Ignatius J. Reilly, I was happy to be away for a couple of days.

About 1:30 a.m., I was awakened by a thud outside. Immediately alert, I listened keenly. "Let's go in here," I thought I heard someone say to another. I froze with fear. My heart thumped, and sweat poured down my forehead. My palms were slick. I didn't know what to do. I wanted to use the phone near the bed to call the police, but if whoever outside heard a voice inside, I feared they would barge in. So I lay quietly as I could, thinking even the sound of my racing heart might be enough to alarm them.

All the warnings of my mother to be careful in New Orleans dashed through my mind and broke my confidence. *Why did I stay here? What the hell?! Why couldn't I rouse myself to scare them off?* Berating myself and swamped with fear, I waited, ears tuned to the slightest sound—a creaking here, a soft murmur there. "Naw we can't go in 'dere,'" I heard. The whispering stopped. Another dull thud outside. Then silence. I remained perfectly still for what seemed like an hour, though I must have been only a few minutes. I didn't sleep but neither did anyone barge into the house.

My friend found the story frightening, offered some encouragement about my doing the right thing (I hadn't done anything!), joked about my profuse sweating (it was no joke), and we went back to talking about our future lives.

"I'm going to take a sabbatical and travel," he told me, "and after that I'm going to make a decision about whether I'm going to stay in the priesthood."

I told him I wanted to find a place to live on my own.

Although the episode at my cousin's house scared the hell out of me, I nevertheless wanted to move away from my parents' home. I wanted to begin life more or less on my own and in my own place. And I wanted to be with folks nearer my age. Uptown, near Audubon Park, Tulane, and Loyola University fit the bill. I found a small garage apartment behind a beautiful Victorian home on Webster Street.

I still wasn't sure what I wanted to do, but since I had majored in psychology at St. Ben, I considered finding work connected to that field might suit me. As a seminarian, I had been both the object and the subject of much armchair psychology from and about my peers, so my new aim was to formalize that informal training. And maybe I could still "help people." I thought having a background in philosophy and religion could make me more empathetic.

Following that path of possibly pursuing an advanced degree in psychology, I took a job as a psychiatric technician in an adolescent wing of psych hospital only a couple of miles from my apartment. Once in the job, I realized that my duties sometimes included more brawn than brain. When the adolescents lost control and threatened harm to themselves or others, they were "coded," which meant they had to be placed in restraints in an isolation room. Restraining patients fell—unfortunately—to the psych techs.

Most of the kids on my unit had various behavioral or developmental problems, some of which could be lessened by mild medication and cognitive therapies. I remember well, however, when a sixteen-year-old paranoid schizophrenic was admitted to our wing. Large for his age, his size facilitated his ideations of grandiosity. One evening I politely asked him to join the group for recreation (something paranoid schizophrenics shun). He kicked over a chair, puffed his chest above me (he was slightly taller than me) and shouted, "You are NOT going to tell me what to do." He was right; I wasn't.

I displayed no agitation, though my heart thumped heavily. He threw the chair, and the nurse on duty, who had heard the display from her station down the hall, coded him. It took at least five psych techs to subdue and restrain him, including a very large fellow from the adolescent wing across from mine. The poor kid writhed and screamed, pulled at the restraints, and scared even his attending physician, who had arrived for an emergency visit. I felt like the hapless techs from *One Flew Over the Cuckoo's Nest*, ashamed that we had to resort to such a measure. It seemed medieval. But had we not restrained him he might have harmed me, the nurse, or himself. I often wonder how he has fared in these nearly forty years.

This fellow needed help, surely, and I felt a bit in awe of the attending physician who worked with him, trying to talk to him about his behavior while also prescribing for him strong doses of psychotropic drugs. The program at St. Ben had emphasized humanistic psychology, so the use of psychotropic medication in the case of this young schizophrenic patient seemed excessive to me, but I knew nothing, of course.

Although this patient stands out because of the severity (and clarity) of his illness, I remember two young girls around fourteen years old: one diagnosed with borderline personality disorder and the other whose formal diagnosis I've forgotten. I looked up borderline personality in the *DSM (Diagnostic and Statistics Manual)*, but had a hard time grasping its meaning. Many of the symptoms could be attributed to adolescence itself:

> A pattern of unstable and intense interpersonal relationships characterized by alternating between extremes of idealization and devaluation; identity disturbance; impulsivity in spending, sex, substance abuse, reckless driving, binge eating.

Others included recurrent suicidal behavior, chronic feelings of emptiness, or inappropriate or intense anger.

Much of this seems par for the course in young people, and thus a diagnosis is not easy.

The other young woman developed a type of "father" transference with me that her therapist used in her treatment. I joined a few sessions, listened and watched attentively, but offered little comment. Apparently my "reticence" was part of what troubled the young woman about her dad, and the therapist used my silence to show her that silence did not indicate lack of caring or disapproval. I'm sure I've simplified the issue, but that is how I understood it then.

I saw this particular young woman a few years later when she worked as a stylist at a haircut chain. As she cut her customer's hair she glanced my way in the waiting area time and again: Was she worried that I did or didn't recognize her? Eventually, I offered a friendly wave but didn't speak with her. I didn't want to put her in an embarrassing position of having to explain a past she may not want to talk about with her coworkers.

At the psych hospital, I saw that the difference between so-called patients and non-patients, except in rare instances, is thin—that nearly everyone manifests behaviors that might be considered neurotic or self-destructive, but the frequency and severity of those behaviors tilt the continuum one way or the other. That, and the support system any given person might have—family, education, housing, insurance.

༄

My mother, ever concerned about what I would do with myself, tried to arrange any number of relationships for me. She happened to be at my new apartment when a woman technician from the telephone company set up my phone line. "She's cute," my mother said. "You should ask her out." When I didn't, she set me up with one of her friend's daughters, the same friend, not incidentally, with whom she travelled to see me when I was in Rome.

My date was easy to be with and kind. We saw *The Big Chill* together, and, later, over pizza, she told me she was put off by the proxy sex in the film. She also spoke of her father, a brilliant research chemist, who had died a few years earlier. She missed him, she said, and spoke proudly of his accomplishments, one of which, I think, had to do with the invention of polyester.

I recall an outing on the sailboat owned by my mother's same friend. The friend's other, older daughter was a med student, already dating someone. The med student wore a skimpy, revealing bathing suit. My mom's friend later apologized to my mother, saying, "I'm sure Eddie was embarrassed by that swimsuit." My mother, to her credit, acknowledged correctly, "I'm sure Eddie enjoyed that swimsuit."

I suppose stereotypes can be useful, but I found that folks pigeonholed me because I had been a seminarian. Most, like my mother's friend or the fellow on the flight home from Rome, thought sex (or a skimpy bathing suit) an inappropriate subject for former seminarians. Whenever I started to discuss certain ideas that ignited my imagination at St. Ben or in Rome, liminality, for example, or the admixture of faith and doubt, most people could not have cared less, so I came to see such topics as "off limits," and kept conversations light.

But other things were squarely in the domain of "ex-seminarian." At family gatherings, for example, I was almost always called on to say grace. My mother, thinking I had a good ethical background, once asked me what I thought about what she considered immoral behavior of her friend's son-in-law. He wasn't cheating on his wife, but he'd regularly gather with his coworkers, all professionals, to watch pornographic films. Odd that she had to ask. I was also asked to offer a public prayer at a family gathering after the funeral of a cousin about my age who had committed suicide. Like everyone at the gathering, I felt horrible about the suicide, I had not expected anyone to ask me to pray publicly and felt put on the spot at such a momentous time. In hindsight, I realized my feelings should not have been paramount at such a time.

I was between the seminary and an unknown future, and "being between" didn't fit the molds into which I was placed by well-meaning friends or family.

᛫

Many years later, while toasting Ben and Shannon at their wedding, I was more accustomed to not fitting in. In my remarks, I made several references to Fyodor Dostoevsky's discussion about love in *The Brothers Karamazov*. Love, he said is not a sentimental feeling, but "hard work." Like a teacher in the front of a class, I kept an eye on the gathered crowd and noticed that my brother Mike and sister Jerrie looked at one another, whispered something, and giggled. I suppose Dostoyevsky might be a little "heavy" for a wedding, so perhaps a little poke at "the professor" was called for. Or perhaps it was continued competition, on my part *and* theirs. I was mildly annoyed, but the occasion took precedence, buoyed also by a greater sense of comfort in my interstitial family space.

On the adolescent unit adjacent to the one where I worked, I took note of an attractive young woman, Denise. She had short stylish hair, creamy tanned skin with a light reddish glow, and a warm smile. When I worked the 3 p.m. to 11 p.m. shift, a group of us often went to Cooter Brown's, the Ur bar for what would soon become the craft beer explosion. At this time, craft beers were few, so Cooter Brown's served beers from around the world.

We'd drink a few beers, throw darts, and talk about work. I found myself delighted whenever Denise joined the group, and somehow, I managed to ask her out, though I don't remember how or precisely when. We dated for a few months. I took her to a New Orleans Saints football game, and she invited me on a family trip to Houston, where we visited my brother Harvey and his wife, Renée, and later stayed at a hotel in the Galleria Mall and attended a Houston Astros game. Though I have never much liked shopping, she managed to get me to stroll the mall with her.

She thought I was handsome and I thought she was beautiful. She made me feel wanted, and seemed to offer me a sense of direction. Since we were both working at a psych hospital we shared a concern for others while enjoying each other's company. I could see a future for us working together in some area of psychology.

She lived in a basement apartment not too far from mine. After work, or on weekends when we didn't work, we spent long hours talking and kissing and making love. *My goodness,* I thought, *here in her arms is the best place for me.* Having had little experience with women, I found myself infatuated. And feeling somewhat guilty at the pleasures we shared—but not guilty enough to stop!—I thought I needed to make our relationship "right."

My mother was pleased that I had found someone. She might also have been relieved that I had cast off a "gloomy disposition" I had fallen into because I didn't know what I wanted to do. Alive in the throes of new love, and happy, I proposed.

My mother came with me to help me purchase an expensive engagement ring, and Denise's parents planned an engagement party at their home in Metairie. I remember very little of that party, for which my family flew in from their parts of the United States—Mike and his first wife, Jan, from Phoenix; Polly and Jim from Denver, Harvey and Renée from Houston, Debbie and Joe from Lafayette, and Jerrie and Don, also from Houston.

I couldn't gauge their thoughts about me or Denise. They had their own lives with young children and came to this party I think out of support and happiness for us.

Unfortunately, a mere few weeks after we said our goodbyes at the engagement party, the happy life between me and Denise soured.

The things I found so attractive about her began to annoy me. She wanted me to be as stylish as she was, so she bought me some "Guess" jeans, very expensive, I thought, and somewhat wanton. The label adorned the fly. When my father saw it he said, "That's a strange place to put the label."

Denise asked me to get an expensive haircut, and continually spoke about clothes and shopping. I had been reading Walker Percy, felt drawn to his thinking, some of which included what he called the "consumer self"—the self, feeling empty, filling its emptiness through consumption. I tried to talk to Denise about it, but she couldn't understand my concern.

We spoke at cross purposes. There were absences from each other's apartments, and when we did see one another, long silences. I called the engagement off one night after a visit at her parents' home. I don't know that anything in particular happened that evening. We had trod clumsily and fitfully for a few weeks, and I had a nagging sense that she was trying to make me into something I wasn't. I don't even remember what I said to her. But whatever I said made us both cry. She tore the engagement ring from her finger, threw it onto the driveway, and ran inside.

So ended my first attempt at being "serious" with a woman.

In retrospect, the relationship would never have lasted. She wasn't a reader or thinker, and I was intensely both, probably too intensely! I couldn't exist on the plane of what I considered her superficiality and she couldn't tolerate my judgment. I mourned the loss and renewed my gloomy disposition, this time accompanied by a mild depression.

I saw leaving Denise as a type of leaving the seminary. Neither was a "failure," but feeling low, I saw both as such, which left me feeling lost and wondering if I would ever be able to commit to someone or something. *Firmum est cor meum?*

I felt myself in a dark forest, with no apparent passage into the clear.

～

Not long after, I entered therapy to try to sort through my place in the world. I had never been in therapy, though spiritual direction had some "therapy-like" qualities. And a religious sister in Rome working on a PhD in psychology spoke with seminarians from time to time as part of her clinical training. We were required to see her. I didn't mind, finding her thoughtful and kind, but I didn't feel a need to see her. So, this voluntary therapy was my first experience with the process. I thought I needed someone to speak with—someone who might give me a more "objective" view of myself, who might help me determine why I had done what I had done thus far and how I might move forward.

I had no breakthroughs of the sort found in movies—I don't even recall most of the sessions. So, I really can't say much about the efficacy of the time I spent. I appreciated the chance to speak about my parents, but I don't recall what I said. It was easy to talk about my struggles with celibacy, but I had done some of that already in Rome, both with Larry and with classmates. I don't think I came out of the therapeutic relationship that much better off than I had when I entered it.

I do remember one thing. At some point during a session, she mentioned, somewhat offhandedly, that she thought I was afraid of success.

I had never heard that before. "How can one be afraid of success?" I thought. "Who's afraid of success?" For so long, I had equated success with "meritocracy"—a good job, a house, a family, the high regard of peers, but I don't think that was the success she meant. I think she meant it as something less tangible—a sense of relationship, of the struggle for person and taking the steps necessary to become more oneself, whoever or whatever that person might be.

Several months later, I met another woman with whom I was soon smitten and who, it became clear, could help me succeed in just such counterintuitive ways.

7

[A]nd soon now we shall go out of the house and go into the convulsion of the world, out of history into history and the awful responsibility of Time.

–ROBERT PENN WARREN, *ALL THE KING'S MEN*

NOT LONG AFTER MY break-up with Denise, I left the psych hospital and took a job with DHL, the courier company. I had become friends with the husband of the head nurse on the unit, and he headed the DHL operation in New Orleans. The company was starting a new domestic service for the delivery of urgent documents on the same day, and he asked if I were interested in manning the office. I didn't think of the move as "permanent." I still thought I might pursue psychology, but I wanted to make a little more money and I thought I'd try something different for a while.

I was sent to San Francisco for training, where I first experienced a taste of "corporate" America, something even back then I thought I could not stomach. It just seemed devoid of of "heart," which I had found in my pursuit of the liberal arts and theology. It all seemed rather monotonous, with a single goal of profit, made possible by appearance and money. Still, I gave it a try.

Fax had not yet been invented, and email was relatively new. I became the office manager in an office of about 1200 square feet. I had no employees, so the only person I managed was me!

Two IBM PCs with two accompanying desks and attached printers looked small in the vast, lifeless, space, but the computers held magical powers. Only a year or two later, those powers would be available widely. The year was 1984, however, and PCs were new!

Recollections on a Road Between

The idea of this new venture was that contracts or other documents could be sent via DHL's network of PCs in large cities across the country, printed out, and delivered within hours. It sounded cutting edge. However, instead of delivering documents, I spent most of my days alone in the huge space, reading, writing, or playing "Wildfire" on the PCs. Occupants of the other offices in the building walked by hurriedly and purposefully, and they offered friendly though wistful waves at my inactivity. Clearly, the idea sounded better than the actual need. I may have delivered three or four documents during my time there.

Though the job offered no career path, I stuck with it for nearly a year. I liked the extra income and the time for reading and writing. And though I thought graduate school still lay in my future, I was not as clear on what I might study. The opportunity for reading and writing made me think I might be better suited for philosophy or literature, though psychology still seemed the most "practical" route for me.

In the spring, I met my old roommate from my freshman year at LSU, René deLaup, at Cooter Brown's. René had been a classmate at Walker. Slight of build, somewhat sinewy, and very bright, he was born with a cleft palate and had chronic nasal problems in his teens and well into adulthood. He sniffed constantly, cleared his throat at least two or three times a minute, and spoke with a nasally, sometimes hollow, voice.

After LSU, he went to Tulane law school. Instead of going into a law firm or into corporate law, he freelanced, researching and writing briefs. A good writer and consummate logician, René had a good legal mind, and could argue about almost anything, parsing the meaning of words, challenging folks like me, who might be less precise in their use of language. It could be fun or it could be maddening, and as he grew older, he became more argumentative and more easily offended when someone counter-argued. He also became frustrated when his interlocutors shied away from his penchant for turning an everyday conversation into a quasi-legal argument.

I had not maintained much contact with him after I entered the seminary, but we reconnected when I returned to New Orleans, especially after I got my apartment on Webster Street. We lived on opposite sides of Audubon Park, which made it easy for us to get together from time to time.

About six or seven months after my breakup with Denise, he called to say we ought to get a beer so he could tell me about a woman I should meet.

Amidst the music and the loud voices and the clanking of glasses at Cooter Brown's, René had to raise his voice. "She's a real looker, Eddie," he said with a barely audible sniff.

"How do you know her?" I asked

"She hung out with us at LSU after you left. She dated Jim and Sam."

One had been a classmate from Walker; the other was the brother of another classmate. I knew them both, but not well, although Jim joined the group for Friday-night basketball from time to time.

"When she left LSU," he continued, "she went to Ohio State and got a Master's in English. She's teaching at UNO now."

"She sounds smart," I said.

"Yeah, she's smart," he said, clearing his throat, "but she was kind of rough on Jim and Sam."

"What do you mean?"

"She just kind of dumped them unceremoniously," he said.

I can't remember what I thought, but having split up with Denise a few months earlier, I could sympathize with this unknown woman. Maybe those guys just weren't for her. Besides, I had come to see that René, ever supportive of male friends, sometimes placed undue blame on women.

"What's her name," I asked?

"Jan Fluitt," he said. "She's got a Fulbright to teach English in Italy."

"Hmmm," I said, "that's a big deal." And I thought to myself, *She must be really bright, maybe a little intimidating. Maybe that's why things went south with Jim and Sam.*

"Yeah, I thought you two should meet."

"Yes!" I said, and asked him if he could introduce us.

He agreed, happy in his role as matchmaker, and happy to join us for our first meeting.

⁓

Jan lived in Mid-City not far from City Park and Bayou St. John—an older section of New Orleans. Most of its regal mansions had been divided into apartments. Jan lived in a small place on the third floor of such a house on Dumaine Street. René rang at the main entrance, and Jan buzzed us in and told us to take the stairs. We knocked on the door.

When she opened it, our eyes met, and I think we both momentarily froze. This is not a romantic exaggeration. René had told Jan that "Eddie's a pretty good-looking guy." She looked at me and I looked at her, both of us delighted (relieved?) that René had told us the truth about one another. Jan wore a white tank top that revealed lovely tanned shoulders. She invited us in, but dropped her keys. She hurriedly retrieved them and let us walk by.

We made small talk for a few minutes, both nervous, and left for Tavern on the Park for a drink. An afternoon shower came through. She said how much she liked the smell of rain. I told her I did too. She had an air of tough aloofness, likely won from her recent breakups, and that attracted me as much as her shoulders. We spoke freely, without too many awkward pauses. The Tavern was closing to prepare for its evening fare, so we left for a bar on Magazine Street.

I don't remember our conversation there. I'm guessing we spoke of her work, my dead-end job at DHL, our backgrounds, and folks we might know in common from LSU or Walker. I do remember that despite my nervousness, I also felt at ease with her, though also awed of her accomplishments. I learned, for example, that she would do more than "teach English" in Italy, as René had told me. Her Fulbright was part of a special program funded by the Fulbright organization (funded by the U.S. government and in partnership with the Italian Ministry of Education) for training Italian teachers of English in high schools and middle schools. She had done so much in so little time. I didn't think I had done as much.

In any case, I certainly wanted to see her again, so I invited her to my place for dinner. When I left Rome, my friends had given me a cookbook called *Roma in Boca*, which had a great recipe for spaghetti alla carbonara, and I wanted to show off my Italian chops by making it for her, accompanied with Est, Est, Est, a popular white wine from Orvieto.

A few minutes before our agreed upon meeting time, I walked down the stairs from my apartment and through the narrow alley to sit on the front steps of the main house to greet her. Fifteen minutes passed, no Jan. *Where was she? Had I got the time wrong?* Thirty minutes. *Had I said something I should not have? Has she decided to dump me already? Why?* I wracked my brain for reasons. *Was it because I had been a seminarian? Had I moved too quickly? Not quickly enough?*

She could have at least let me know. Forty-five minutes!

Deflated and a little miffed, I walked back up to the apartment to give her a call. No answer. Well, so much for this first date.

While I was wondering what to do with the food I had bought, she finally called me to let me know she was on her way and would arrive in another fifteen minutes. *Wow! That's still pretty late!* But at least she called. Annoyed but happy with anticipation, I went back down to wait on the steps.

She pulled up in her brown Toyota Corolla station wagon and promptly apologized.

Ah, good manners after all, I thought judgmentally!

"I was almost to your apartment," she said, "when I decided to fill up my car on Magazine Street. I overfilled the tank, and gas got all over me. I smelled like a gas pump!"

She went on to say that she reeked so much that she drove back to her apartment to shower and put on fresh clothes.

"Ahhh," I replied, grateful it wasn't me after all. "Well, let's go upstairs."

We walked up the stairs to my place. I offered her some wine, we chatted (about what I don't remember, most probably about her upcoming Fulbright), and I made the carbonara. After dinner we sat on the steps at the front of the house and had a couple of more glasses of wine before she left.

Hooray! Success! She even kissed me!

Well, this was a new feeling! A smart woman who seemed to like me! And though she was headed for Italy in a few months, we had those few months if we wanted them.

Later, we met at a place on St. Charles Avenue. I was talking about my reading—by this time, I had read a collection of interviews with Walker Percy. I used these interviews as an "entry" to understanding Percy's fiction and nonfiction, and I read his works in light of what he said about them in the interviews. I spoke with Jan about the excitement I felt in reading Percy's works, that he seemed to address concerns about the "self" (my-"self")—about me, my own experiences, my woundedness. She looked off to the distance, and I, thinking she wasn't listening, said, "I should probably stop talking because I'm boring you."

"No" she said! "It's just a habit I have when I'm thinking about something. I look away. Keep talking."

So I did.

We saw each other several times after that, and we talked of family and books—she liked George Eliot and Lillian Hellman, writers about whom I knew nothing. We talked about family, LSU, and a year she had spent in Montpelier, France, between college and grad school.

She had been fluent in French, though now it was a bit rusty, and since she was heading to Italy, she wanted to learn some Italian. She asked if I would tutor her. "Sure," I said. Though my Italian was decent, I had never been fluent, and I had left Rome two years earlier, so what I retained was evaporating quickly. Could I live up to her expectations?

She was moving out of her apartment in a few weeks, however, so we had to plan around that.

One day, I got a call from Jan at my empty DHL office. "I think I'm obsessed with you," she said.

Never, ever, had anyone said anything like that to me. I wasn't sure what to make of it. I liked Jan, but the intensity of our growing relationship frightened me. "Obsession" scared me. I don't remember what I said—again one of those big moments you'd think I'd remember, but which has been sifted out of my memory somehow. Because of fear? Because of joy?

René told me "the word on the street" was that Jan had fallen for me. I called a good friend from Rome, Carl, who had, a few weeks before I met Jan, come to New Orleans for a visit. Quick witted, smarter than he would admit about himself, and funny, he joked, "I wish someone were obsessed with me!" My priest friend from Notre Dame, who had one foot out of the priesthood by now, told me he thought I might be "rebounding" with Jan after the breakup with Denise.

I liked Carl's assessment more than the idea of rebounding, which I didn't believe. My feelings were strong, and though I was afraid (of commitment? of where our relationship might go? of my lack of clear direction while Jan seemed on an upward trajectory?) I knew I liked Jan too and wanted to continue to see her.

Since she would be leaving in the fall, Jan hadn't renewed her apartment lease. Some friends of hers from UNO were taking an overseas vacation, so Jan agreed to watch their lakefront home while they were gone. By this time, we had met for three or four tutoring sessions, went out for beers or dinner, and we felt more at ease with one another.

I helped her clean up her place on Dumaine. The apartment was empty save for a few small boxes. We sat on the hardwood floor, practiced a little Italian, and chatted. What I remember vividly about that day wasn't the cleaning or the lessons in Italian. It was the kissing! We didn't do anything more than kiss and tumble gently on the hard floors, but oh my, that was plenty enough! What a delight!

Long live obsession—hers, and now mine too!

Later she invited me over for dinner at her friends' home. She met me at the door in a yellow sundress. Though I said nothing, I mistook the dress for a short nightgown. (I'm sorry to say that my mistaking items in Jan's wardrobe continues!) She had bought the sundress while in Provence. Her shoulders, tanned and fit, drew my eyes, as did the looseness of the dress, which allowed periodic and furtive glances of her unbound breasts. We poked around the house, looked at books on the extensive bookcase, kissed on the study sofa, and no doubt had dinner too, though I don't remember what she served. I remember, as the time drew near for my departure, she looked me softly in the eyes to say, "If I asked you to stay, would you?"

Heck, yeah! I thought, but controlled myself enough to say a simple, "Yes." I felt happier than I had been in a long time.

The route to the lakefront house grew familiar. We took twilight walks (Jan's favorite time of day) to the steps at Lake Pontchartrain, talked, held hands, kissed, and dreamed about a future neither of us could quite imagine. She was set to leave in the fall, which fast approached. When we weren't at the lakefront house, she came over to Webster Street. The summer passed in a blur of lovemaking and talk—about her impending departure, what we might do, how we might make it work, even in Italy.

One night at my place, she asked me point blank if I would join her in Rome. More aware of what such a step would mean for my relationship with my parents, not to mention the commitment it implied, I hesitated. She grew very angry, grabbed my shirt, announced that I had lied to her, and collapsed in tears. A bit later she regained composure. But she had scared me. She had challenged me to commit, and I wasn't sure I was ready. Fear of success?

In the next few days, indecision whirled. I spoke to Carl, my friend from Rome who resided in St. Louis, and Chris, both of whom listened without judgment. I spoke to René, but don't remember what he said. Jan and I talked and cried and talked more. We agreed finally that I would visit her in early December, and I would return to live with her after the holidays.

Jan left in late September. We stayed in touch daily. Email wasn't available then, so we wrote letters almost every day. We telephoned and spoke far too long. When I got a phone bill for nearly $500, we decided that we needed another way to communicate. We would let one another know we were thinking of them by means of a code. Call, let the phone ring three times, hang up, call again and let it ring once and hang up again. That served as a transatlantic "I love you," and didn't cost a cent.

Our letters were detailed, effusive, and copious. We both saved what the other sent, and for our first wedding anniversary, Jan bound them together chronologically. We read them each anniversary for several years. As the obligations of family life and work increased, however, we pulled them out only to find ourselves somewhat embarrassed to see ourselves as we were. We've debated whether we should discard them. I don't think we should! They stand in witness to our mutual obsession, despite our youth, the flowery effusiveness, and sometimes lascivious detail. While we are not the persons we were, the letters nevertheless capture vividly our breathless longing. They remain a gift!

Jan was the better, more concrete writer. I tended to offer quotations from what I was reading or tried to fit what I was feeling into more abstract ideas. For example, not long after she arrived in Rome in mid-September 1985, Jan wrote:

> Eddie, I feel so good in this city; it really feels like home to me and I think it's because I feel your spirit here. But not just you—*we* are here together. It only makes me sad that I can't physically touch you as well as feel you. Soon, Soon.

One of my first letters to her, which probably crossed in the mail with the one I quote from above, noted the following:

> We had a beautiful Sunday here in Ole N'awlins. It was to me the first indication of fall. The air was clear, clean, and crisp. The sky was that deep blue which indicates a lack of humidity. In all, I felt the onslaught of those "feelings of eloquence, omnipotence, and yet sadness for the state of the world and its inhabitants" [a quote from one of my own "early poems,"]. Indeed I felt on top of the world.

In another, written 30 minutes after our first transatlantic call, I say:

> The 30-minute talk we had seemed much less than a half-hour. Alas, time without you is time slowed by the action of memory and anticipation. Time with you is that of fullness and love. I miss you terribly.... Jan, how wonderful it would be to be with you [in Rome]. My heart pounds more quickly even as I write it.... Soon I will "come to you and be your love." (Excuse the paraphrase. I don't think Donne would mind.) How I wish I could roam the Borghese with you.

Early in our letter writing, we began signing off with "Je t'aime, Ti amo, I love you."

Recollections on a Road Between

~

After the first burst of enthusiasm, Jan went through a difficult period of insomnia and work-related disorganization. Assigned to the South of Italy, she was supposed to live in Naples. But she couldn't find housing there and returned to Rome, where she ultimately found an apartment on Via Domenico Silveri, ironically behind the Janiculum Hill and NAC—"just left of the Vatican," as we said then and for years after. She hadn't begun work even a couple of months after her arrival.

Difficult times found counterbalance in her getting to know Larry, who took her out to eat at some of our old haunts and introduced her to Rome. She also found companionship with Beth, a second-year Fulbrighter who had picked her up from the airport and oriented her to the city and to the job. Beth would become the putative leader of the group we came to call years later, the "Roman Ladies."

In early December, I flew to Frankfurt with a courier pass from DHL. I had arranged vacation time so I could visit with Jan a couple of weeks after dropping off DHL's packages in Frankfurt. I could hardly stand the short flight from Frankfurt to Rome, knowing Jan awaited.

She stood in the arrival parlor in a blue knit sweater-dress with boots and a large black belt. We kissed, hugged, and walked arm in arm to a taxi for the ride to her apartment. Snow covered the umbrella pines and the monuments, something I had not seen before. Everything seemed magical, as though the ancient city had adorned itself for our reunion.

We arrived at Via Dominico Silveri and took the stairs up. The apartment was tiny, without room even for a kitchen sink, but it didn't matter. I felt at home there immediately. We walked over to St. Peter's square at dusk. Nearly empty because of the cold and snow, we frolicked like kids, threw snow balls at one another, kissed near the obelisk, and left our shoe prints in the snow-covered grand piazza, as though saying, *We are here!*

I don't remember all that we did during those two weeks, but I do remember Larry came over for dinner one night, his large frame dominating the corner where our small table rested. He and I finished nearly an entire bottle of Averna. I remember walking to Piazza Navona, lined with Christmas booths, the smell of roasting chestnuts (no kidding!) in the crisp air. I remember a dinner with Beth and others at the apartment of the Cultural Attaché from the American Embassy and another gathering of other American diplomats or expats. I remember dinners out with Larry or just us two at Trattoria la Maddelena near the Pantheon and Cecilia Matella on the Old Appian Way. I remember walking in the Villa Borghese, through the Piazza del Popolo, down the via Babouini, and to the Spanish Steps. All was well. We talked about our plans for living together in Rome in the New Year and what we might do with our futures.

Jan had planned a trip home to see her parents between Christmas and New Year's, so when I left after my short visit, we knew we'd see one another again soon. I spent Christmas with my family and Jan with hers, but just after Christmas I drove up to see her at her parents' house in Brandon, Mississippi, north of Jackson. Jan's mother, a pious Catholic, had come to see me as a "gift from the Holy Spirit," a role that, perhaps true, nevertheless felt ill-suited. Though they didn't approve of our plans to be together after January, they seemed to offer us a pass since I apparently had won them over in ways some of her previous boyfriends had not.

I had not yet told my parents (who liked Jan) that I planned to live with her in Rome, and I wouldn't have, had they not asked one day a couple of weeks before my departure: "When you go to Rome," my mother asked, "where will you stay?"

With fear and trembling, heart pounding, I said, "With Jan." A short pause, and then "Where did you think I would stay?"

My mother's face dropped and her eyes welled. My father, never one to express his feelings easily, sighed deeply.

"I thought you'd stay with Larry or get an apartment with one of Jan's male friends," my mom said plaintively, as though it were obvious, but layering her voice with pain and concern and a jab of guilt.

"No," I said, trying not to sound too forthright, still trying to please, "I'm going to stay with Jan."

"This is the hardest thing I have ever had to deal with," my father said, having been silent until then. This coming from a man who had served on a warship in the Pacific during WWII and who had steered ship and crew through a typhoon! Not to mention, furthermore, having raised seven children, steering them through the tumultuous 1960s and providing a good living for them.

I knew they would be displeased, and I displeased them. I had broken a family pact, I felt, not living up to the high standards they set for everything—performance in school, performance in the world, performance with one another. And though I knew I had hurt them, I thought truth needed its say.

When I was leaving, my mother said, with some anger and dismissal, "I hope you find whatever you're looking for."

For at least a year, I was a *persona non grata*. Some friends and family told me my parents wouldn't even mention my name when I was gone, so much did they disagree with what I did. For the eight months or so I was with Jan in Italy, I heard from them only once. The very short note, written by my father, was an Easter card addressed to me. At the end he wrote, "Hello to all."

My brother Mike also sent a note that said I had been "too honest" with them. He meant well, and wanted to offer support, but I didn't think fibbing my way to avoid their hurt and anger would have worked for me—or for them.

Though fearful, I also felt liberated! I had not gone through a "break" with my parents as some kids do far earlier in their lives. I was now twenty-six years old, by most standards an adult. Nevertheless, I was the son of my parents, who had raised me—consciously and unconsciously—to live by the values they set, to obey the church in sexual matters, and to respect family. I knew by moving in with Jan I violated all three. At the same time, however, I also felt that I needed distance from my parents. Perhaps I displayed a late-adolescent rebellion, an attempt to differentiate myself, to "succeed" on my own terms. I knew I wanted to be with Jan, knew I wanted to be in Rome, and still wished to remain in the church.

Would the God of the universe condemn me for having found happiness with Jan? I had already stepped across the "no-sex-before-marriage" line, and I could not imagine that cohabitation would damn me.

I realize that my status as an "almost priest" might have aggravated the stain I now brought upon my parents. That same status, however, opened me to the possibility of recognizing grace, an openness together with Jan to a vision, though clearly counter to official teachings of the church and in clear violation of my parents spoken and unspoken interpretations of those teachings, of something large and unknown—in the interstices, in the spaces between the rules of church and family and my and Jan's transgressive longing for one another.

⇜

Jan and I thought it would be a good idea for me to set up a small business of serving as a typist and editor of papers for students at the various universities while in Rome. I bought an Apple computer and a daisy-wheel printer. I learned how to use the computer while at my desk for DHL and set up the printer at home. In those days, mapping a printer to a computer took a level of expertise and time I didn't have. René knew more about the growing digital world than I did, so he came over to help set the printer so that it would talk with the Apple.

I placed the printer and computer in a leather bag (one, ironically, my mother had purchased for me at the leather market in Florence when she visited me at NAC), and I used it for my carry on. The bag was heavy, and my hands ached when I carried it for more than a few minutes, but I muscled through the airports in New Orleans and Atlanta, and finally Fiumicino, where Jan awaited.

In that tiny place "left of the Vatican," Jan and I set up "home." It would be the first of many.

⁂

Larry remained a good friend during our time in Rome. Unlike some of my potential clients (seminarians doing graduate study), he didn't judge—or if he did, he kept his thoughts to himself.

Jan had begun working and travelled to the south for days at a time. Larry and I went out to eat as we had when I was a student. He took Jan and me out to dinner when he could and allowed us to use his car from time to time.

I would like to say our days in Rome brought constant bliss, but that wasn't the case. Jan and I tested one another's patience and identities, and like newlyweds, we set boundaries and threw each other off balance. I continually worried about money (part of my male need to "provide"), so when Jan once splurged on a bright-yellow pleated skirt, which by the way looked great on her, I chastised her for spending wantonly. Not my finest hour.

And I tended to sing in the shower. At the time, I was stuck on old St. Louis Jesuit hymns I had played on guitar thousands of times at Masses. Jan thought I was trying to catechize her through the songs, which brought a torrent of reproach to match my chastisement of her spending.

Would we, could we, last? If there was a breakthrough, I don't remember. I tried to temper my comments about spending and I quit singing in the shower. She understood the centrality my time in the seminary had played in my life, and began to appreciate more the intellectual underpinnings of religion, something neither she nor I had appreciated growing up Catholic. And we persisted.

Our days filled with work, reading, cooking, and visiting. Still thinking I might pursue a career in psychology, now as a Jungian analyst, I read several of Carl Jung's books, admiring his combination of myth and the unconscious mind. We read Dostoyevsky, Melville, Steinbeck, and others and discussed them excitedly.

We came to know the other Fulbrighters well. Beth, who had extended her stay, had a head of light brownish-blond curly hair. She liked to tell stories, eat, drink wine, and laugh. She became the axis of the small group of Fulbrighters we came to know, along with Maria, who had stayed in Rome after her time expired and who lived with an Italian boyfriend; Helene, assigned to Florence and whom we visited a few times and who came to visit us in Rome; and Sally, who, though not a Fulbrighter, had graduated from Fordham University with a law degree, worked a couple of years, and was taking some time off to experience life in Italy. She returned to the United States with an eye toward returning to Rome, which she did in 1985. She's been there since. Despite our various backgrounds and the insecurities and posturing of our youth, we managed to form bonds that have lasted more than forty years.

These friends became the "Roman Ladies." In a fractured, divided world, such friendships are rare. Jan and I are grateful that our original link with these smart, capable, and fun-loving people has endured through marriages, divorces, and relocations. We find ourselves at ease with one another in the simple mystery of friendship amidst the ineluctable passage of time.

The Roman Ladies at our 40th anniversary gathering.
Saint Coulomb, France, September, 2024.

Recollections on a Road Between

Jan and I celebrated Beth's thirty-36th birthday with the group of Roman Ladies and Luigi, the deputy director of the Fulbright Program in Italy. We drank, we laughed, we sang Happy Birthday and *Buon Compleano*. We felt unconquerable, in the world but somehow apart from it, happy despite the trials of new life together, a future with one another looking more and more likely.

Jan and I, with Maria (a "Roman Lady") and her then boyfriend at Beth's 36th birthday celebration. Rome, April 1986.

A few weeks later, we took a train up to Orvieto. We walked up to the walled city with its striped Duomo. While we wondered at the story of salvation told by the spectacular bas-reliefs of its façade, we viewed skeptically the blood-stained corporal, the miracle of which supposedly "proved" the mystery of transubstantiation—a host having bled onto the cloth. We walked through the pottery shops, had lunch at a small *trattoria* (with Est, Est, Est of course) and finally made our way to a lookout at the northwest corner of the city wall. I knew what I had planned, but I didn't know if Jan knew. I was nervous, but ready. As we gazed at the colored blocks of Umbrian farmland toward the Tuscan hills, my heart thumping and stumbling over the words I had rehearsed internally, I asked Jan if she would marry me.

As you already know, dear reader, she said "Yes!"

Despite our penchant for not being sentimental, we laughed and marveled at our good fortune to have found one another and love—and to celebrate it in this tiny medieval city overlooking a broad expanse of the Italian countryside.

We talked of getting married in Rome, but decided against it, mainly for logistical reasons. It would have been too difficult to have the sort of "family" wedding our folks would expect. Surprisingly (or not) I have no recollection of calling my parents to let them know the news. Surely I would have, since Jan had called her family. I don't know if a frigid reception of the news stymies my memory or if residual anger has blocked it—or if I called them at all.

Larry delighted in the news and offered to officiate.

Jan and I in Morano Calabro. Southern Italy, June 1986.

Jan's Fulbright ended, so we bade farewells to Sally, Maria and Antonio, Beth and Helene, and flew to New York City to stay with one of Jan's college friends who now lived and worked there. We stayed a few days before returning to New Orleans, to what we knew would be a difficult re-entry.

We knew we'd have to face my parents head on, so we called them from New York, let them know we planned to return to New Orleans, and asked them, full of dread, voices trembling, to meet us at the airport in New Orleans. They agreed! First "good" sign!

As it turned out, however, our luggage was lost. *Damnation of damnations! Why now?!* Here we were, returning on a high, yet full of misgivings about a reception we knew would be fraught. My mother had a long, solemn face. My father seemed as nervous as we were. As we waited for word about our luggage, conversation started and stopped, mostly stopped. The silence filled with unspoken hurt, judgment, and the anxiety of trying not to let those feelings get the upper hand. The ride to my apartment was no better.

Jan and I lived together at Webster Street for a short time, but eventually found half of a shotgun on Jena Street, very near the triangular intersection of Fontainebleau, South Broad, and Napoleon Avenues. The arrangement didn't sit well with my folks, but because we actively planned marriage, it stung them less. My father happened to know our landlord, another oilman, who lived next door. Knowing the landlord somehow made Jan and my arrangement better in my father's mind, though he was far from sanguine about it.

One day, as Jan and I continued reparations with my parents, we visited them on Mimosa Court. At the breakfast table, my father, who thought I should go to law school, grew impatient with whatever small talk we were making. At one point, somewhat out of context, he blurted out, "Everything would have been just fine if he [meaning me] had stayed in the seminary!"

Never one to miss a chance for righteous argument, Jan sat up in her chair, looked him directly in the face and with raised voice said, "Well, he did leave the seminary! And now he's here."

I don't remember what I said, if anything. I resist confrontation, particularly with my family, having learned the deep arts of internalization—probably not the healthiest of coping strategies. Content to let Jan argue on my behalf, I remained silent.

Later, I told her that I couldn't recall anyone in my family having confronted my father so bluntly. She said, "Well, they should have!"

Jan and I experienced our own strains as well. On a late-night drive back from Baton Rouge, we degenerated into a shouting match, an argument so intense I had to pull over to the shoulder of I-10. I turned on my flashers as our shouting gave way to tears. I can't remember what issue could have caused such passion, but I recall a sense of anger that had bubbled up from days or weeks of repression.

As we tried to sort things out, I saw flashing lights pull up behind us. A young Louisiana state trooper, knocked on the window and asked if we needed help. Somewhat embarrassed, we glanced sheepishly at one another and told him we had "domestic problems." He nodded in sympathy, told us it would be best to get off the highway, and let us be.

Around that time, Jan and I saw *The Mission*, the film with Jeremy Irons, Robert DeNiro, and others about the Jesuit Mission to the Guarani people near the Argentine/Paraguayan border. C.J. McNaspy, S.J., a quirky and brilliant Jesuit priest who for years taught music at Loyola University, had written a book on which the film was based. He had come to St. Ben when I was a student to lecture about that work and his study of Egyptian hieroglyphics. The film's eclectic, stirring music accompanies a story of lust, love, betrayal, murder, penance, forgiveness, natural beauty, music, and the fecklessness of a Christendom too willing to sacrifice the indigenous Guarani to the corruptions of church and state. I was deeply moved by the film. We walked out to the suburban mall parking lot in stunned silence. When I got into the car, we began to talk about the film—or tried to. I began to sob as I had not done in years, if ever.

It could have been the metaphorical expression of sin and forgiveness, shown majestically by DeNiro's character climbing a waterfall with the instruments of his slave-trading past and allowing the mission's leader to cut the rope by which they clung to him. It could have been the innocence and dignity of the Guarani, who lived peaceably in primal beauty, accepted music and education and the Gospel as brought to them by the Jesuits, and whose faith outshone even that of their teachers. It could have been a feeling of my own lost innocence or recognition of a faith I couldn't express or live up to.

In the years since that evening in my car in the dreary suburban mall parking lot, I have connected those sobs to dreams that have recurred during my life with Jan and our children. While they vary in content, the dreams carry similar structures and emotions. I find myself in the seminary, somewhat dislocated and shaky (what else?), yet preparing for a public function of some sort: a homily, a test, a presentation, an ordination (my own or others). Wracked with guilt and feelings of inadequacy or cowardice, I never quite meet the moment, whatever that moment might call for. I am revealed, broken. And I awake confused, shaken, mildly depressed.

I see these dreams not as an indication that I *should* have stayed in the seminary, as my father told Jan long ago. I see them, rather, as tied to fear of commitment, a lingering self-doubt, and signs of the countless witting and unwitting compromises made at the altar of self. Could I, like the Jesuits with the Guarini, create beauty and fight for it (and them) when confronted with injustice? Can I stand up for the poor and oppressed? Am I, as St. Paul called Peter, a "reed blowing in the wind?" Can I accept my fallen and broken nature, accept forgiveness as something given and not earned, accept the brokenness of others and shun foolish pride—self-centeredness, self-sufficiency, self-importance, self-this or self-that?

You who now read this must know that I am naught without you. We are responsible for one another. Our lives, inextricably bound in time and memory and history—broken, fragmented—nevertheless connect by this narrative, a glimpse into an evanescent and frightful-joyful passage—the passages that comprise my story.

Jan and I married on January 10, 1987 in the small chapel in Christ Court at Saint Joseph Seminary College. Larry officiated and Fr. Scott, one of my spiritual directors at St. Ben, and who had hired Jan to begin the ESL program at St. Ben, assisted. Jan's Aunt Faye and my friend Br. Justin Brown (later Abbot Justin) served as lectors. Sean Duggan, a young monk and winner of the international Bach Piano Competition, played the piano at our reception. The wedding was a joyous event!

Jan and I with Larry Bronkiewicz, my spiritual director from Rome and officiant at our wedding. Larry is godfather to all our children, who call him "Uncle Larry." St. Benedict, LA, January 10, 1987.

My parents were delighted, as though a switch flipped inside of them. We who had been unmentionable were suddenly "speakable," and not just speakable, but worthy of celebration. A picture from our wedding day shows them carrying flowers from the chapel after the wedding. Their smiles expand nearly to the edges of the frame.

Jan and I with my family after our wedding in the small chapel at St. Joseph Seminary College. St. Benedict, LA, January 10, 1987.

Mom and Dad walking with flowers after Jan and my wedding.
St. Benedict, LA, January 10, 1987.

Jan and I spent our wedding night, appropriately, at Maison Dupuy in the French Quarter (a gift from Larry). The next morning, when we pulled up for the after-wedding party at my parents' home, my mother's happiness startled Jan. Mom opened the door and offered a big smile and a bigger "Hello." Jan turned around to see if my mother were addressing someone behind her. But she wasn't. My mother's hello was for Jan and for "us," now legitimized in her eyes by a sacramental union, family balance restored. I, in her eyes, no longer lost.

8

Touch a limit of your understanding and it falls away, to reveal mystery upon mystery. The one great lesson we can take from the study of any civilization is the appropriateness of reverence, of awe, and of pity, too.

—Marilynne Robinson, *The Givenness of Things*

Even before the wedding, Jan and I had discussed what direction I might take with further study. Her position at UNO prodded me to think about an academic career for myself. And while I was still attracted to psychology, the time we spent reading and talking in Rome, coupled with my "alone" time in that DHL office of one and a short stint as a medical editor at Ochsner Foundation Hospital had opened me to the idea of going to graduate school in literature.

Unlike many scholars or writers, I had come late to the value of reading. Certainly, St. Ben and my theological studies had opened me to seeing myself and the world very differently. Most of that change I attribute not only to the self-reflection that formation required, but also to the power of the liberal arts. Though I wasn't particularly well-read, my experience of reading and writing about what I read had changed me. I wanted more, and so I applied and was accepted into the graduate program in English at LSU.

Jan had been hired to begin the ESL program at St. Ben, so we moved to Hammond, Louisiana, about equidistant between Baton Rouge and Covington, so that she could begin her work and I could begin my studies.

It was a heady time of reading, researching, and writing—the creative years, I like to call them, not only because were we creating new (between) spaces for ourselves, literally between Baton Rouge and Covington, for example, but also because we lived between scholarship and the demands of family. Our three kids, Benjamin, Madeleine, and John, were born in May

1989, December 1990, and October 1992 respectively, during my time in grad school and Jan's new position.

We moved to Covington just before Benjamin was born so Jan could be closer to work and to the baby. That first summer with our first born was great fun, made more delightful by Benjamin learning to sleep through the night at seven weeks! We moved again just before Madeleine was born nineteen months later. Although we stayed in that house until John was born (twenty months after Madeleine), we needed more space, so we moved yet again. Three children (and three houses) in a little more than three years!

How we did it, I don't know. We had strict schedules, as though bells regulated the rhythm of our days. Ding, time to wake up. Ding, breakfast time. Ding, nap time. In the evenings we had dinner, gave baths to the kids, put them to bed (ding, ding, ding). Then Jan and I talked awhile before I went to my study to work, often eating chocolate-covered coffee beans to keep me going until 1:00 or 2:00 a.m. Then (ding) we'd start all over again around 6:30.

Of course, the babies got sick, sometimes all at once, and the well-regulated schedule fell to pieces. John had persistent ear infections that required several sets of ear tubes. Madeleine seemed to have nasal infections constantly, and her reaction to antibiotics could result in astonishing bowl-movements. Benjamin fell at his second birthday party and cracked his upper front teeth, which had to be removed. Chicken pox or everyday colds and coughs disrupted sleep and often made Jan or me sick as well. But we learned in concrete fashion to accept messiness. The liveliness of these burgeoning persons, moreover, bursting with discovery and mischief, made our lives more full than we might have ever imagined.

My parents helped often, as did Jan's, both financially (we were not making much money) and with babysitting duties. I wrote the third chapter of my dissertation in about a week, just after the birth of John, when Jan's parents came down from Jackson to help us with Benjamin and Madeleine, then about two-and-three-quarters years old and twenty months, respectively.

Before the dissertation and before comprehensive exams, but not before the idea of them, I remember walking into the bedroom at 2:30 a.m. with a crying Madeleine in my arms. "I'm going to have to postpone my comps," I told a weary Jan. And I did.

After Madeleine's birth in December of 1990, Jan dropped to part-time status. She was still teaching, but the monks allowed us to set up our schedules so that we didn't need day care. John was born mid-fall-semester of 1992, so I picked up Jan's classes after he came, while also teaching at LSU and working on the dissertation. Still, one of us was always home with the kids, a real gift.

At my PhD graduation with Jan and our children: Benjamin (4 years old) in front, Madeleine (2 years, 4 months old) in Jan's arms, John (7 months old) in my arm. Baton Rouge, LA, May, 1993.

Making babies and researching unveiled a new sense of the world, myself, and my in-between place in it. But I came to see that odd space more as a given. I dove into research on Kierkegaard, Heidegger, postmodernism, and theorists of autobiography, not only James Olney, but Paul John Eakin, Janet Varner Gunn, Georges Gusdorf, and others, all with an eye of showing that Walker Percy's novels and essays tread similar, but different territory.

Recollections on a Road Between

Because we had three babies in the house, I was particularly drawn to Walker Percy's language theory, especially his semiotics of self in *The Message in the Bottle*, the ideas of which found distillation in *Lost in the Cosmos*. At the beginning of language recognition, children receive the name of a thing as a summons to retrieve it—a ball, for example. Later, the child understands that the word "ball" doesn't mean "get the ball"; it means the spherical object with which one plays. Percy writes that a two-year-old goes around the house naming things, finding joy in the knowing that names bring. Percy's key insight maintains that consciousness comes from the Latin, *conscio*, which literally means "to know with." This argument stirred me. In naming, one knows, and becomes "conscious of," a thing with another and places it in the world. A community forms between speaker and hearer.

When the two-year-old becomes a seven-year-old an odd thing happens. The child, conscious of a peculiar entity, a self, discovers that the self, unlike much of the world, has no name that applies. And thus while a child can know and "place" things in the world by pairing them with names, because the self has no name, its placement is, at best, problematic. And this displacement, first experienced at an early age, remains.

It is no wonder that Percy used Nietzsche as an epigram for his trenchant, hilarious book: "We are unknown to ourselves, we knowers." In my studies, I came to see that autobiography is always an attempt to name the self through the passages of a text, a combination of time, memory, and narrative. But whatever self emerges is always and already "between." There's always a gap between the passages that make up the text and the passages that form lived experience. And while a gap exists, say, between the word "pencil" and the wooden thing with which one writes, one still knows and places a pencil in the world in a way one can't know and place one's "self."

And so "self" quite literally finds no place, no home. It exists "nowhere"—in that space between past and future, the present, which continually looks backward (in memory) and forward (in anticipation). Though "self" often capitulates to the boundaries established by culture or family or career, self is more than any of these. Self requires a continual "presencing," nowhere but also "now, here" in the spaces that poetry or story or art or music name, in genuine religious experience, in the act of knowing with, finding out, and naming in science, and in the deep longing that arrives unexpectedly in any possible instant—as as it did for me while listening to an impish uncle sing "Delta Dawn" on False River or hearing the mournful strains of Copland's "Night Waltz" from *Rodeo*, or on a dimly lit via Julia during a music festival in Rome, on the golf course, at a movie, in dreams, the birth of a child, a reunion with a lover.

※

I didn't have such a full view of my work when I wrote as a graduate student under the deadline of three children and little money. Rather, my troubling over issues of place, placement and home, reflecting on having moved the family many times over for work or schools, and now, here, writing at a small desk in a room still partially full of boxes from our last move, I see more clearly what I only guessed at during the writing of my dissertation.

Later, as a college administrator, when I talked with fellow administrators about their grad school experiences and their dissertations, they often said they had no interest in their dissertation. Some said they were embarrassed by it, suggesting, perhaps, a recognition of sloppy or un-nuanced scholarship. Some said they did it simply to fulfill a requirement of graduation. I felt a bit odd, because although I readily admit that my research may not have been as thorough or as finely argued as it could have been, I still thought it was relevant, at least for me! I had continued to mull it over (as I do now) years after its completion.

I saw my research and writing as a continuation of the explorations I had begun as a seminarian. For me, writing was a question of finding a name and a place for this strange encounter with the restless, unsettled, and nowhere space that was myself, obviously among others, and sharing with Jan the responsibility of a small family.

※

In one of her many interviews, Eudora Welty noted that "children growing up now have lived in five or six houses by the time they are ten years old." She said this in 1978.

From 1989, the year Benjamin was born to 1999, he had lived in five houses. From 1990, when Madeleine was born, to 2000, she had lived in five houses, and from 1992 to 2002, when John was ten, he had lived in four. In that same interview, Welty was asked if she thought so many moves made children "rootless and restless." She said, "I suppose, and every place is getting somewhat alike. In the future, it's not going to be the same, but I think there will still be a deep sense of family to people who have grown up with that" (*Conversations with Eudora Welty*).

In another interview she noted that writers are interested in whole characters, and that life in a small town, such as her fictitious Morgana, Mississippi, allows you to see the arc of a life, more or less from birth to adulthood.

We certainly didn't stay in one place. A friend's mother called us "nomads." Another friend said he thought Jan and I were probably the "least rooted" people he'd ever met. He didn't mean we were "unhinged," at least I don't think he meant that. He referred, I think, to our many comings and goings—a sort of restlessness that came about from our continual moving from place to place.

Getting ready for one of our many moves!

Despite our nomadic life, Jan and I nevertheless created a sense of family. And we've had the great good fortune of having seen our children grow up—from birth to their regulated stage as infants and toddlers (ding!), through the trials of adolescence, and then to schools and colleges and into their lives as spouses and as parents themselves.

How to find the right words to describe the arc of their lives so far?

The early weeks and months pass in a blur of feedings, diaper changes, and naps. For me it was its own in-between time: an extraordinary fatigue accompanied by wonder at a creature so fragile and dependent, yet sturdy enough to have passed from womb to world.

Then the explosion of mobility, crawling, scooting, walking, the beginning of exploration, coordination, differentiation, limits, and eventually language, naming.

As they grew, I began to see myself reflected not only in physical appearance, but in mannerisms—a frown, a smile, a gesture, a gait, a laugh. Later, I saw other, perhaps less obvious traits—sneakiness, fibbing, competition, determination, will—and I was buoyed that we could form them while also frightened at seeing so much of my ill-formed self I thought less apparent to others.

Ben was a happy baby, good sleeper, and compliant companion as he sat in his baby bouncer while I read Melville or Faulkner, gently bouncing him with my foot. He loved to walk, to explore, to pull things out of cabinets. A tow-headed toddler who loved activity, loved moving things—cars, trains, trucks, school buses, garbage trucks—loved touching things, putting them together, breaking them apart. Played soccer and tee ball, and later flag football. Smart, he sometimes struggled to focus on school work; a late reader, but always a good communicator. He ran cross country in high school and became team captain. Like most teenagers, did some things we didn't know about, pushed back against the limits Jan and I tried to establish. Stayed with a "surrogate family" to finish high school in Montana when the rest of the family was in Savannah. Was accepted to Georgia Tech, felt somewhat out of place among what he called "nerdy braniacs," but persisted and made long-lasting friendships. Got a paid internship in Seattle, where, after some tumult, he eventually met his future wife, Shannon, environmentalist in the progressive PNW. Now a husband and father, social, handsome, articulate, still active (mountain biking, skiing, running) still touching things, building things, and taking them apart, and teaching his daughter, Rylan, to follow suit.

Madeleine, who challenged us even in the womb, when Jan developed an enlarged corpus luteum cyst, difficult to diagnose, but which caused searing pain when it folded over her uterus. Cyst removed by aspiration, an experimental treatment, Jan's pregnancy moved forward. Due on December 7, Madeleine waited until December 22 to arrive, but came hurriedly after Jan's water broke. A beautiful baby! Willful even as an infant.

Had trouble nursing, trouble sleeping. Became a willful toddler insisting things, like tying her shoes, be done on her schedule. Entertained herself with a strong imagination, became fascinated with Egyptian art early on, which may have led to her love of cats later. A sophisticated, droll sense of humor even in middle school, telling visiting grown-ups that "intelligent male" was an oxymoron. Her willfulness did not decline in high school, a period of adolescent angst and rebellion. Went to UGA and became fascinated with the environment after a study abroad in Costa Rica, which led to graduate studies in Biology (entomology, conservation, and plant science), married an artist/designer, James. Teaches environmental conservation in the community college system in Washington. Mature, articulate, a loving spouse, beautiful, thoughtful, still strong-willed, but a will directed more toward others' good and the mission of teaching students who have had less opportunity than she has had.

John, the lightest but longest of our three babies. Happy, even with chronic ear infections as an infant and toddler. Woke up a bit loopy after one surgery and asked when it would start. A peace maker—a glue—between Ben and Madeleine. Fascinated with Troy Aikman and Emmitt Smith when very young. Somewhat unhappily, played Little Guy football in Montana, broke an ankle playing basketball in middle school. Attended a small high school with an International Baccalaureate program in Savannah. Excelled academically—history, math, even Latin. Went to UGA, had to be convinced to take a study abroad program in Rome (with enthusiastic support from Jan and me), met a fellow UGA student on the program, Lindsey, who eventually became his spouse. Went to UNC-Chapel Hill for a graduate program in Computational Physics, got the master's degree, took a job with a software company. Migrated to Washington, where he works remotely, with Lindsey, who works in conservation communications for the state. Thoughtful, somewhat quiet, but also eager to have a conversation. Already the "favorite uncle" of Rylan, and now he and Lindsey are parents too, of Eli, born in the late summer of 2024, a beautiful baby boy.

While the arcs of Jan and my lives bend gently toward the earth, the arcs of our children's lives ascend. They are grounded, however, with their spouses and with one another. Jan and I marvel at our good fortune. Despite many jobs, many moves, and many houses, despite a fractious and fractured culture, despite the specter of restlessness and the possibility of rootlessness, we have, somehow, despite ourselves, continued to foster a sense of home, a sense of family.

Recollections on a Road Between

In 1994, however, the year after I graduated with the PhD, and about a year before a revised version of my dissertation came out as a book, we found ourselves amidst unexpected family fractures, the initial strains and stresses of which go back to a much earlier time in my story.

9

Before the mountains were born
the earth and the world brought forth,
from eternity to eternity you are God.
You turn humanity back into dust,
Saying, "Return, you children of Adam!"...

Seventy is the sum of our years,
or eighty, if we are strong;
Most of them are toil and sorrow;
they pass quickly, and we are gone.

−Psalm 90:2−3, 10

In the summer of 1982, I studied Italian in Siena, Italy, at the Dante Alighieri Institute. I was there for six weeks of intense, advanced classes, since at the Gregorian University in Rome instruction took place in Italian. I loved living in Siena—the great piazza in the center of town, the narrow streets, the *contrade* (small urban districts within the city, each with its own church, museum, and history, usually named after an animal: eagle, she-wolf, giraffe), the shadows of the Borghese family cast nearly everywhere, palace intrigue built into the cobblestones.

I lived in the large upstairs room of a family home rented out long-term to students. One of the things I remember most about the apartment is that one of its windows opened onto a very small piazza. Each night, Sienese from the *contrada* in which the apartment stood (I don't remember from which animal it took its name), gathered for a video showing of *Il*

Palio, the famous horse race that takes place in the grand piazza of the city. Their *contrada* had won the race this year, and so a group from this small area of the city relived the ecstasy of the win each night, projecting the race onto a wall of one of the piazza's buildings. A full night's sleep rarely came.

While in Siena I received a long letter from my brother John, unusual since he hardly ever wrote and since I believed the Italian post could not be so efficient as to get it to me before my language course finished. In the letter he told me that he had come out as gay to our mother, who, as I have said, was a staunch Catholic.

Nevertheless, our mother loved family as much as the church. She and John cried together, he wrote, because they were happy to have found such a bond in the truth. He said he had known he was gay since he was in middle school, though he hid it from everyone and felt obligated to do the things "ordinary" middle- and high-school kids did, like go to prom with a girl. I found out later the girl he took to prom knew he was gay before anyone in our family and agreed to support him in his secret life. "I am tired of having to hide who I am," he wrote.

Despite such honesty, he and Mom decided it best not to tell Dad, who had strong opinions about how life should be lived. Remember the placard of the dog on the bar in our house in New Orleans! What would he do with such news of John? Fun loving, but also impatient and quick-tempered, he expected us to toe the line. And he could give a look that could make you want to crawl under a rock.

"I'm writing you now," John went on, "because I know you will understand." I read through the letter several times, happy to be entrusted with this semi-secret, but fearing for him and the family nonetheless. AIDS among gay men had been in the headlines awhile. In fact, the Centers for Disease Control marks its inception as June 5, 1981.

I suspect John knew that many seminarians were gay, and thus I had knowledge of living with those who had been, like him, fearful and isolated because of their sexuality. I remember sharing the letter with a friend from the seminary. He took the occasion to tell me he was gay and of his own struggles at being so. I could relate, simply because of my own struggles with sexuality, which by comparison had been less complex, but still troubling.

John finished Centenary in 1984, playing collegiate tennis throughout his four years. After college, he went on to medical school at the LSU School of Medicine in New Orleans, graduating with the M.D. in 1988.

Recollections on a Road Between

I don't recall the year, perhaps 1986, John called to say he had been diagnosed with HIV. I asked if he had told Mom, which he had. They still didn't say anything to Dad, who, if he had suspected anything about John's identity, said nothing to me or to our mother. By this point, John had "been out" (at least partially) for about four years.

John lived disease-free for a few more years, which allowed him to finish med school and begin a residency in dermatology. In the summer of 1989, while completing a residency in Houston, he called to let me know that he had been diagnosed with tuberculosis and was in the hospital—the first presenting illness of his HIV AIDS. He knew the time had come to tell Dad and the rest of the family.

Jan and I hopped in our little Honda Civic, baby seat in the back for Benjamin, who was only a few months old, and set out for Houston. We stopped in Lafayette, where my sister Debbie and her husband Joe lived. When they asked why John was in the hospital, I told them bluntly that John had AIDS.

Debbie gasped and then cried; Joe tightened his lips and held tight to the counter top. I had a great sense of release in having spoken it. The Dupuy family, as I have said, is not good at addressing matters head on. Although we spent a good part of the rest of the evening recounting the history of John's secret life, I can't recall ever having spoken about it with them again. Perhaps this is my own "Dupuy-ness," part of my penchant for avoiding difficult topics.

Mom made the step to tell Dad. I don't know how she approached him, and I don't know what, if anything he said to her when she told him, but our misgivings about his nature proved unfounded. He did not fly off the handle. He went to Houston to visit his son, where, though not very communicative, he offered support for his sick child.

We think we know our parents or those we love, but maybe we know only our image of them.

When we were at the hospital, we were told to wear masks and gowns, not because of the AIDS but because of tuberculosis. I remember when Jerrie, our oldest sibling, arrived at the hospital room. She walked in, eyes wide with fear above her mask. We were all afraid, of course, as was the entire country. This disease killed people left and right. At the time, AIDS was a death sentence, and our brother had it.

After John was released from the hospital, we took Benjamin to visit him. John held our baby boy in his lap, a proud uncle, surrounded by Mom and Dad and those who had been able to get to Houston on short notice.

On the drive back from Houston, we visited Jan's favorite aunt in Baton Rouge, Aunt Faye, who had read one of the scripture passages at our wedding. Her husband was an LSU law professor and they used to come visit us when I was in graduate school when we lived in Hammond. We loved their visits—Aunt Faye, who was funny and smart; Uncle Warren, who liked beer and bourbon, and who liked to hold forth. We shared many a good Sunday afternoon with them. When we stopped to see her on our way back from Houston, her oldest son was visiting with his first baby. We told the story of having visited John in the hospital.

Nothing was said then, but Aunt Faye called us a week or two later and told us that they could no longer visit with us. Nor were we welcome in their home.

What? Why? Stricken and mystified, we were more so when they told us it was because of my brother's AIDS.

Didn't they know better? AIDS is not communicable through the air. But the hysteria surrounding AIDS defied reason. It was a time not unlike the global COVID pandemic, when misinformation, contradictory directives, and a politicized public hindered a measured response to disease, especially in the United States.

John recovered from tuberculosis, got a job as a staff dermatologist with Kaiser Permanente in Los Angeles, bought a home in Hollywood Hills and lived the California life, complete with a Saab 900 turbo convertible.

We didn't see Aunt Faye or Uncle Warren for nearly ten years. Jan's father finally intervened with his sister to say enough was enough. We happily reunited.

⁓

Polly, the second oldest, got the best of the looks of Mom and Dad. She was blond, blue-eyed, and thin. She had a Mary Tyler Moore innocence about her that played into her image as an "All-American" girl. I always thought she was my dad's favorite. She was homecoming queen for the University of Southwestern Louisiana (now University of Louisiana at Lafayette), and I remember Dad beaming as he stood for photos with her.

Recollections on a Road Between

Polly graduated with a BSN and moved to Houston with Jerrie. There she met a young Englishman, now a Canadian, Jim, who was working in the oil patch for Texaco. Jim had been a runner with Olympic potential before a broken foot derailed that dream. He was funny, energetic, a bit irreverent, something of a braggart, and a convert to Catholicism—exotic for a young woman from South Louisiana. Polly must have dreamed of romance and travel. They moved to Calgary, Alberta, soon after marriage, and she bore my parents' first grandchild there. I remember taking a long road trip to see them and the baby. At the time, 1974, it was only my second time out of the country, if a day in Juarez, Mexico, with Uncle Ed and his family counts, and the first time to see the Canadian Rockies, which left an indelible wrinkle in my memory.

They later moved to Denver, where I visited them in 1983 after having left the seminary. I remember watching *Aliens* on a laser disc system Jim had bought for the family. In one scene, Sigourney Weaver, wearing only a T-shirt and underwear, closed a hatch or a bin on the space craft—her rear end nicely framed in the shot. "Welcome to the real world," Jim said. Polly demurred. I remember driving with them on a snow-covered road on the way to cross-country skiing. The car slid from time to time, and Polly would tense with an inhaled hiss. Perturbed, Jim said, "Don't worry, Lovie, I've got control even if you can't feel it."

A geophysicist by degree, Jim made repeated attempts to strike it big as an owner of an independent oil and gas company. Through the years, he set up several companies and tried to steer them so that they would be swallowed up by a bigger fish for a good price. Although he provided for the family, his dreams never worked out the way he'd hoped. It took a lot of bravura to do what he tried. He was not averse to risk. But Polly was. And their differences were not always complementary.

My father, who worked for Chevron for 45 years, climbed the corporate ladder, did not understand why Jim left the stability of Texaco. To him, Jim's brashness, drive, and failure to strike it rich turned his efforts into a sort of morality story—stick to the tried and true, and you'll be rewarded. My Mom began to think Jim wasn't upholding his duty to care for Polly or their three kids, a sentiment reinforced when the oldest child began to dabble in drugs.

Sometime in late 1993 or early 1994, Polly was diagnosed with breast cancer. The small cracks between risk and control widened, and the morality play progressed to a bitter, pathetic end. Exhausted and depressed from months of radiation and chemotherapy, Polly chose an Independence Day soccer tournament—when she knew Jim and three kids would be out of the house—to hang herself by a rope in the basement of their suburban house in Littleton, Colorado. She had researched how to tie the knot. Imagine the horror of discovering your wife or mother's lifeless body hanging in the basement of the family home.

Jan and I got a call from my mother early on the morning of July 5. "Polly died yesterday," she said, her voice resigned and tired. "What? What do you mean?" I asked, my mind racing. "She killed herself," my mother said even more sadly. Our minds reeled.

We had only a few days before suffered a loss of our own.

⁓

Jan and I used to joke that we were so fertile that we shouldn't wash our underwear together. While we had not planned to have a fourth child—in the summer of 1994, Ben was five, Madeleine three and a half and John one and a half—we nevertheless welcomed another pregnancy and began preparations for a new baby in the household. Familiar with the routine of prenatal care, Jan went in for a regular doctor's appointment at twenty weeks pregnant. She was by herself when the doctor tried to find a heartbeat through her stethoscope. I was with the kids and Uncle Larry, my spiritual director from Rome, who was visiting. Jan met us after her visit. In tears, she ran toward me to say that something might be wrong with the baby.

When the doctor could not find a heartbeat, he recommended that Jan travel to a facility in New Orleans that had a sonogram machine. In the examination room, the technician moved the probe from top to bottom, side to side, listening for the baby's heartbeat. Jan asked anxiously whether there was a heartbeat. The technician said, "I'm not going to lie to you; there's no heartbeat." Not allowed to make a diagnosis, the technician called in the doctor, who confirmed the bad news. We had so looked forward to another baby in the house.

Jan and I were left to consider the next steps: a D and C that would remove the remains of the fetus and allow Jan's womb to heal, or a "natural miscarriage" that could take weeks or longer. Sad enough already, we didn't want Jan to have to carry a lifeless baby any longer. We scheduled the D and C.

Jan was about five months into the pregnancy, and as with the other pregnancies, we had decided not to find out the baby's sex. We had named this baby Francis, gender-neutral, and a name that recalled a trip we had made to Asissi when we were together in Rome.

We asked the doctor if we might be able see the remains of Francis after the procedure. She was clear that the baby was still tiny and that after the procedure, very little of Francis would be intact. We wanted a way to mark this loss, however, so we held a small memorial service attended by some good friends and led by one of our monk-friends from the Abbey. It would, we thought, provide a sense of closure for the short life of a child we never saw, except in our anticipation, but who nevertheless marked our lives.

⁓

Polly's breast cancer diagnosis added to what was already a tense situation in the family. Jim's latest business was not doing well, and he was trying to find a way to exit and begin again. Polly went through chemo and radiation and the long recovery from both. She fell into depression, which proved serious enough that Jerrie went to Denver for a visit and to help.

She later told me, with the guilt often felt by relatives of a suicide, myself included, that while she was there, she could tell Polly was depressed but she didn't realize how depressed she was. I had written Polly a letter, and a friend of hers told me later that the letter almost got through to her. What more might I have said?

My parents also went up to help. While they were there, I recall a phone call from Jim saying that my parents were driving him "fucking" crazy. Clearly, everyone was on edge. Polly was depressed, my parents were stressed, and the pressure of it all no doubt built up, with little release.

My parents loved Polly and Jim and their three kids just as much as they loved all their grandchildren—and great grandchildren.

In 2011, long after the events of 1994, our family celebrated my mother's eighty-fifth birthday in Austin, Texas, where Jerrie and Don had bought a house and where all their kids and grandkids lived. At one of the gatherings at Jerrie and Don's house, there must have been at least thirty extended family—my brothers and sisters and their spouses, their children, and in some cases, their children's children.

I saw my mother standing to the side looking pensive.

"What are you thinking about?" I asked.

"Look at what we've made!" she said, wonder and pride and love in her voice and her hand extended toward the room, full of noise and motion and laughter.

This was my mother's attitude toward family.

In 1994, however, while caring for Polly, a different side of her shone forth.

Like many people, my mother could express dissatisfaction by means of a drawn face or a sigh. She had another especially effective way. Whenever she disapproved of something you did or said, she would make a sound that existed somewhere in the region just before locution, something like "Oanhh." It was a bit nasally and hollow and drawn out just enough. I suspect she directed several "Oanhhs" at Jim and the kids.

And no doubt my father's "motor was running." When my father was preoccupied, he'd hum, flap his lips and exhale, all at the same time, sometimes changing pitch as though singing. It was a totally unconscious habit. While putting Christmas decorations back in the attic or paying bills, his motor might run effortlessly, but when preoccupied, he invariably started it up.

The manifestation of myriad stressors, I suspect, prompted Jim's comment to me on the phone.

The grandkids, especially Stephanie, the youngest, could not have helped being marked by their mother's suicide. Only fourteen when Polly died, Stephanie later developed a series of maladies affecting her joints, stomach, and muscles, which lead her to pain killers. Bret became a teacher and later director of a small pre-school in Seattle, while David pursued a Ph.D. in comparative religion, with an emphasis on Buddhism.

I know life doesn't lend itself easily to such patterns but it's hard, in the perspective of such a trauma, not to see that Stephanie sought help and attention. Bret cared for children. And David sought solace through religious study. Each was left seeking some sort of sense—a meaning—of what their mother did.

For a time, Mike and his wife Shelley invited Stephanie into their home. They wanted to help, to give her a sense of stability after a few years of grief. She stayed with them for several months. About a year after Stephanie moved out of their house, the family gathered for a Christmas reunion in Denver and the Rockies. Through the years, we often got together as a large group in Galveston at Jerrie and Don's bayhouse or in Destin, Florida, at one of the many condominium complexes.

The last family photos including Polly and John were from Destin in 1993, and they hung in my parents' home where they caught the morning sun. My brother Mike had suggested that each family wear a different colored polo shirt—lavender, aquamarine, denim. Since I was still in grad school and our kids were still small, Jan and I chose white because we already had white polos for everyone and we were too cheap to buy new ones.

My parents kept two large blowups of the photos in their living room—one with everyone, spouses and all the grandkids, and one with them and the "original" Dupuys. The photos remained in their appointed places until, like faded shrines, they were removed after my father's death in 2017.

The extended Dupuy Family. Destin, FL, summer 1993.
The last time Polly and John were in a family photo.

For some reason I don't recall, Jan, I, and the kids could not attend the reunion in Denver. Not long after that gathering, however, we received a letter from Jim. In it, he said he was discontinuing contact with the Dupuy family and requested that we not contact him or his kids. The formality and angry tone masked a deep hurt. I called Jerrie, who was closest to Polly and Jim, to find out what the letter portended.

Jerrie said that things were going well until, as will happen during family reunions, they started talking about the past. Somehow the conversation came around to Stephanie. Mike took the occasion to chastise Jim for his poor parental skills. Jim, in turn, lambasted Mike and the Dupuys for their smugness. I can't remember more of what Jerrie said, but I'm sure that explosion of emotion ended the possibility of further discussion—and likely the gathering altogether.

I can imagine the scene: a conversation spawned by unspoken, repressed, grief turns to blame and ridicule, the opposite of what had been hoped—that is, coming to terms with the loss of Polly, the great white elephant amidst the garlands and lights of Christmas. Unfortunately, grief can't be controlled, and dialogue can be risky, especially for the wounded and those unused to the vulnerability it requires.

Polly's funeral took place at her parish church in Denver. At the wake the evening before, I remember seeing Jim sitting in the back of the church speaking with Renée, Harvey's wife. Were they recounting their experiences of life with the Dupuys?

I remember my mother standing next to the open coffin telling me how "good" Polly looked, but then pointing out the scar left by the rope. Feeling like a child in my mother's presence, I said nothing, could not even muster words to console her, who must have been hurting terribly.

I cried as Polly's coffin was put in the hearse for a trip to the crematorium. Her ashes would be buried later in a Denver cemetery. Jan and I did not see the burial spot again until at least seven or eight years later, returning to New Orleans through Denver from a road trip to Montana. Despite the letter of a few years earlier, we stopped to see Jim at his office, where Stephanie also met us. I asked her to drive us by the home where I had spent so much time with Polly and Jim, and then asked her to take us to her mother's grave.

A flood of memory (coupled with a sense of trespassing) hit me as we walked around the backyard. I had played football or soccer with the kids there. Jim had barbecued there. Polly had laughed. I remembered those days as a whimsical period before the time of pain and sorrow and hurt and grief.

At the cemetery, which we have not visited again, I looked down at the gravestone: "Jessie Pauline Ellerton, January 23, 1948 – July 4, 1994. I thought of the police report recounting the horrible scene in the basement of the home we had just visited. Among the material in the report was a note she had left to her kids: She said she was "proud of the persons [they, her children] were becoming" and was "sorry not to be able to see [them] grow up."

Well, I thought, angry and grieving myself, *she did not NOT have to see them grow up*. But I said nothing.

Had I said more in my letter, found better words, would it have made a difference? Could any of us have altered the act that marked her children's histories and our own?

⁓

My parents left Polly's funeral to take care of John at his house in Hollywood Hills. He was very sick, waking up drenched with night sweats. Tired to the bone, Mom and Dad got up each night to wipe him down with cool rags and to change his sheets.

John flew me out to be with them, and my brother Mike came out for a few days as well. We all prayed with him, the old prayers my mother loved—the Angelus, the Memorare, the Act of Contrition, the rosary. She fed him and us and tried to relax or sleep when he slept. We tried to help with the night duty, but she insisted on getting up.

Sensing that this illness might be his last, I wondered if John had considered assisted suicide. Since I was the "almost priest" in the family, I took it upon myself to comb through some scholarly essays on the "Catholic view" of end-of-life matters and brought them with me.

I recalled Walker Percy's comments in a letter to Shelby Foote in which, after his cancer diagnosis and search for treatment, he mused on the possibility of assisted suicide, ultimately rejecting it because it was "not allowed" by his Catholic faith. I encouraged John and my parents to read the articles, hoping they would not try to take control of the situation. I don't know if they ever read them. The articles were scholarly and dry, so I suspect not.

In hindsight, I think taking the articles with me was my own way of trying to control an uncontrollable, uncertain situation—my way to plead with John not to go down that path. Perhaps it was my way of saying, *Don't leave early.*

But who was I to say what he should or should not do? And would I, in the same situation, not think about the same thing? I could not fathom the depth of his suffering and the perception he had about its impact not only on himself, but on those who took care of him, especially Mom and Dad.

And why couldn't I say anything like this to him or the rest of the family directly?

When it became clear he would not recover, my parents decided to fly him to their home in New Orleans. One of John's friends, an executive in the Disney corporation, arranged a private jet to fly them home. I met them at the airport, along with a good family friend. We took John's bags and his wasting body to their condo that overlooked the Mississippi River at Algiers Point.

The timeline becomes fuzzy for me once John returned home. He may have been there a month or just a couple of weeks, but he grew weaker and more wasted almost daily. He took a cocktail of medications, including Marinol to boost his testosterone production and thus his appetite, and early versions of AZT. Mom could not understand the need for Marinol: "It was testosterone that got him in trouble in the first place," she once told me. But he was too sick for any cocktails of drugs to be effective.

As his immune system continually evaporated, we had to be selective in allowing visitors near him. Jan went in to be with him when I developed a cold and didn't want to infect him. During the nights she was there, he hallucinated and held conversations with whatever or whomever he saw or heard. Jan described it as eerie and spiritual at the same time.

Jan left on September 12, and on September 13, Mike arrived from Phoenix. John had asked him to be with him "at the end." They had a plan that I never knew about and that no one in the family has ever spoken about openly.

Sometime early in the morning of September 14, John died. Once the sun came up, Mike called to give us the news: "John died last night," he said. "I'm sorry to have to tell you. It was a peaceful death."

Jan still recalls what Madeleine told her when we returned from our visit to the doctor: "I'm sorry the baby died in your belly, Mommy."

※

In Abu Dhabi, I used the distance of space and time to remember and to write, as I do again now.

I often awakened before daylight with Jan to hear the muezzin's call to morning prayer. On September 14, 2019, as I listened to the plaintive chant, I remembered that the day was the twenty-fifth anniversary of my brother's death. In the Catholic liturgical calendar, September 14 is also the Feast of the Triumph of the Cross, so my brother's death remains tied to this feast day, when the church recalls annually the paradox of life conquering the sorrow of death, even death on a cross.

The muezzin calls worshipers to prayer five times each day, beginning with "God is great" and ending with "There is no God but Allah." In Abu Dhabi, the calls can seem misplaced because the ostentatious wealth might suggest Muslims there have little room for Islam, which means "submission."

Still, they called, and I felt buoyed by their sound—mournful yet confident, meditative.

Even though I heard the call to prayer thousands of times and have often read them transliterated, I cannot always distinguish the words when sung in mellifluent Arabic. Their indecipherability resembles the deaths of Francis, Polly, and John in 1994. The deaths widened cracks in the family foundation, though they didn't bring the house down. They remind me of the risk, fragility, and what Marilynn Robinson calls "the givenness of things"—things beyond control despite a lingering belief that they can somehow submit to my whims.

And though I have thought about these deaths and their repercussions countless times over the years, I can't always fathom their meaning. Distinct, the deaths nevertheless remain a unit in my memory. I submit to them. And with these words I submit them to you.

In the Christian tradition, the triumph of the Cross finds special recognition on September 14, but Christians are asked to recall and submit to the many daily "crosses" of life.

In his rule for monastic life, Saint Benedict asks monks to "keep death daily before their eyes." He asks them to submit to the "small death" of discipline, to be sure, but also to remember limitation, humility, and the ultimate return to "humus," earth—the place of death, a place residing somewhere between sorrow and triumph.

After John died, my parents had his household items, clothes, and his car shipped to our house on 6th Avenue in Covington. We had a large garage where we put John's clothes and household items, and we parked his Saab 900 Turbo convertible out on our rock driveway. Taking the kids for rides around town, top down when weather allowed, introduced us to the "caste" system of car ownership, a peculiarity of our culture we had not experienced or expected. Folks who drove Porches or Jaguars gave us a wave, a flash of high beams, or a simple nod of approval. What a strange land we live in!

John had introduced us to the Indigo Girls, so I played their album—*Indigo Girls*—incessantly on the sound system that ingeniously bounced sound off the front windshield so that even with the top down and cruising on the open highway, we could enjoy the music. The melancholy "History of Us" especially captured my imagination. I could hear in it not only the lost relationships that befell us in those three months and their after-effects, but also the very real difficulties of finding "a medium for life"—or death—as I try to do now.

10

I have seen all things that are done under the sun, and behold, all is vanity and a chase after wind.

—Ecclesiastes 1:14

Life, of course, went on.

A revised version of my dissertation was published in January of 1996. I dedicated it to Polly and John.

During the last few years of graduate school, I had sent out hundreds of applications, and though I had a few interviews, I was not successful in finding a teaching job. Because the seminary college approached the time for its ten-year reaffirmation of accreditation, and because they needed a faculty member with a terminal degree in one of the liberal arts, the college offered me a job. I taught a 4-4 load and worked up an evaluation schedule required by our accreditation agency.

This teaching position morphed into my becoming director of communications and later dean. I continued teaching even as I held each administrative position. Including the couple of years I taught part-time while still a grad student, I worked eleven years at St. Ben. In hindsight, the positions I held there, especially as a dean, continued a sort of formation. In the dean's role, I had a hand in helping to shape the academic program, a central part of the formation. Still somewhat young, however, and with a hankering to see new places, I thought I needed to move on. When the president of Our Lady of Holy Cross College in New Orleans approached me after a presentation that I gave to the St. Ben board and said he needed a senior vice president for academic affairs, I jumped at the opportunity.

Young and somewhat ambitious, I knew I needed to make more money, and while I had not expected (or wanted) to return to the neighborhood of my high-school years, I took the job. Being closer to my parents would be good for our kids and for Jan and me, we thought, so we moved to the neighborhood just next to the college that held the office, where I had spoken with Fr. Roy some twenty-six years earlier.

I had thought, somewhat naively, that "formation" could be a part of Our Lady of Holy Cross College (OLHCC) as it had been at St. Ben. To some degree it was, because the college's mission articulated a goal to "educate both the mind and the heart" of its students. OLHCC had more than ten times the students that St. Ben had, however, and it was a commuter college. Students fit in their college work while tending to jobs, to their children, or to myriad other obligations. I thought faculty and students would share an educational vision, as the monks and lay faculty had at St. Ben. And I thought a sense of learning for learning's sake, subordinate to a larger vision of person, might find a place at OLHCC as well.

I knew the faculty and monks at St. Ben well. Some were my classmates and some were my professors, just older. I knew them, understood their personalities, and felt at ease with them and the common cause for which we worked. In contrast, OLHCC introduced me to a more normative (shall I say) faculty and staff, composed of members who had their own ambitions, who had competing visions of what education should be, and some who felt at odds with one another and didn't hesitate to make their voices heard.

Warmly received at first, I soon became the target of darts thrown from a variety of angles. This position, like the one that followed at Rocky Mountain College, was complicated by members of the college leadership (the president or members of the board of trustees) telling me I'd be the next president of the college.

I felt flattered in being told I could step into a presidential role, and yet, I felt torn. I had entered higher education as a seeker, as someone bent on sharing a (still somewhat ill-formed) vision of self as a wayfarer or pilgrim, occupying "between" spaces. I assumed that other administrators and faculty might share a similar quest.

Instead, I often became embroiled in petty politics.

Despite the politics, I found many successes among students, faculty, and administration, especially younger colleagues. These eager colleagues and I sometimes set ourselves against what we saw as calcified practices, probably without enough sensitivity to those who had made them. At times, my ambition hampered the work I did. I found myself at odds with presidents or department/division chairs, or some other senior members of administration, particularly in my first two positions in higher education.

Furthermore, while I have gone to great lengths in my story to suggest a "place between" as my experience of self, I felt uncomfortably torn between scholar and administrator. When I attended administrative conferences, I felt out of place because I thought the real work of education rested in scholarship and the classroom. When I attended academic conferences, still presenting papers at literary meetings from time to time, I thought faculty too naïve about the complexities of administration.

I see now that my attitude was somewhat self-defeating. I dreaded accreditation, for example, and viewed it as an attempt to quantify what I thought an essentially unquantifiable and mysterious practice—education, particularly liberal arts education. However, as a senior academic administrator at small private colleges, the task of leading accreditation efforts fell to me. In spite of my attitude, I successfully lead Rocky Mountain College through its 10-year reaffirmation, and I gained from the state of Texas the authority to grant degrees in the new program in San Antonio.

At Our Lady of Holy Cross College, I was happy to reduce the teaching load of faculty to comply with teacher education accreditation standards. When the professor who wrote that document, however, wheeled in a ten-volume document on a cart, each volume consisting of some 150 to 300 pages, I sighed. *Is this what education was about? Who will read this?* And when the education program presented me with a plaque thanking me for my "leadership" in making accreditation possible—I had done very little, in truth—I felt even more miserable. I hadn't realized that was how the game was played. Only later I realized the source of my misery: a "thanks" tinged with passive aggression.

As senior administrator, I was expected to play by certain rules. I embraced some, such as promoting faculty compensation or funds for faculty development, especially scholarly development, and promoting student success, but the politics of small college administration continually annoyed me, even as I clumsily participated in it.

With a single exception, the colleges at which I worked had enrollments of less than 1000 students. Some, like St. Ben, or the small art school in San Antonio I helped start, had less than 100 students.

No matter the size, however, I came to see that managing a small private college is like trying to manage an ostensibly democratic country. The president serves as the chief executive, presumably executing the broad policies of the board with the vice presidents, principally the VP for academic affairs and the faculty, for the mission to educate students. As experts in their respective disciplines, faculty create and oversee the curriculum, teach it, and have a voice in broader institutional matters, including recruitment and faculty policy.

However, as in any human institution, personal ambitions, pettiness, rivalries, jealousies, and insecurities keep the democratic process highly stressed. The president, often protected by the board chair, falls into autocratic tendencies. The faculty, sometimes feeling cut off from governance, tease out minutiae of policy or curricular matters until they frustrate themselves and the entire president's cabinet. Some, feeling protected by tenure, descend into intellectual lethargy, fussing about parking, or food services, or academic freedom, which unlike today, was hardly under siege at that time.

At one college, a tenured faculty member told one of his students that she should not wear "fuck-me pumps" to class. I found out about it because the student had told one of the other vice presidents, who told me. When I called the faculty member in to discuss the matter, several other faculty members came to his defense, saying I had violated his academic freedom. They brought copies of the AAUP's "red" book, which outlines, among other things, guidelines about academic freedom—none of which say faculty can demean students in class—and threatened to contact the AAUP to investigate my actions.

At a different college, I directed a search for an endowed chair in a key discipline for the school's mission. The president, who had raised money for the chair from a well-known businessman in the community, told me the selection of the chair was my and the faculty's decision. When I made an offer after consulting with the faculty search committee, the president, who had hoped to offer the job to another of the candidates, called our chosen candidate, convinced him, I don't know how, to refuse the position, and I was forced to offer the job to the candidate he had wanted all along.

At still another college, the president fired faculty or administrators, more often the latter, at will. I was unceremoniously let go without warning, even after having received stellar performance evaluations from my immediate supervisor. The wiles of the president prevailed.

A particularly difficult year at another college culminated with the ousting of a president who had hired me. Several board members had told me that they thought I would be the next president. Still ambitious (and a little stupid), I thought I could help take the college out of its morass, although in retrospect, I think I was wrong. The college needed a stronger hand than mine, but my ambition proved greater than my sense.

The drama began at the end of a board meeting at which one of the president's early supporters placed a "vote of no confidence" on the table for consideration. A confused board chair cited the "irregularity" of the motion and tried to move forward "regular" business (at this point the closing of the meeting). The board had already divided itself into camps, however, and the body agreed that more information about the president should be brought to light. They decided to hold a closed-door session at which members of the president's executive team (including me) would present evidence of his "misdeeds" and thus cause for his removal.

The windows of the meeting room were papered over, lest anyone try to illicitly watch or report anything to the press. The board also insisted that the president be in attendance to hear his accusers. The session had the atmosphere of a cabal meeting, a monastic chapter of faults, or ultimately an early American witch trial. Clearly the faults outlined would not be our own, but rather those of the president. Clearly, the only outcome would be his "guilt." The fact of the meeting insured his removal before it began.

The chair of the board solemnly announced the purpose of the meeting. The president's executive secretary, with paper and pen at hand, took minutes. The president walked in and sat in what amounted to a prisoner's box. My stomach had churned all day, but it roiled when my turn to speak came. I had carefully prepared my comments and spoke for about seven minutes, while others spoke from notes for only a few moments.

I had mixed motives. I knew that his ouster could mean my accession to the president's chair. Despite recognizing the need for a change in leadership, I left the meeting with a strong distaste for what had taken place and my participation in it. The wheel of history, however, had been set in motion. The board later met alone with the president and removed him from office. To everyone's surprise, not least my own, the board selected one of their own members to serve as "interim president."

As I grew into the various executive leadership roles at different colleges, I came to wonder at how any institution—national, state, or city government, a corporation, a parish council, a college, a book club, a neighborhood homeowners' association—manages to get anything done at all.

Some thrive despite poor leadership. Some flounder despite good leadership, and some just get by, with good, bad, or mediocre leadership, doing what good or ill they might.

༄

So how do I talk about my career in higher education, one marked by good and bad leadership, my own included? A career marked by opportunities to shape institutions, to shape faculty and students, to shape learning? What I can say is that I had good days and bad days. Some days I thought I contributed to a better world; other days I thought I added to its demise.

I came to see that I was as susceptible to the allure of power and money as anyone else. I saw my own autocratic tendencies, but also tried to mollify them with democratic practice. Although faculty and staff sometimes dropped into complaining pettiness, many rose to share a common vision of passing on to students the opportunities and vision they had themselves been given.

Through it all, I enjoyed working with students in whom I often saw versions of my younger self, eager at the opportunity to soak up new understanding. I enjoyed supporting faculty where I could, despite the scuffles I had with some. I took pleasure in streamlining bureaucratic processes. I also enjoyed the speaking opportunities that came my way.

I became good at interviewing for jobs—mainly because I worked at five different institutions over the thirty years or so of my career. In those interviews I was forced to develop an educational vision, to offer comments on leadership and teaching, to say how I might help institutions change, even if they resisted the change they said they wanted, and to clarify my thoughts on what I saw as the power of the liberal arts.

In addition to interviews, I was called on to give talks to faculty, to student groups, to community "town and gown" organizations. I was asked to write for student newspapers, to give "formation conferences" (at St. Ben), all the while continuing to produce book reviews for scholarly journals and the occasional scholarly paper for presentation at a conference or for publication. In doing so, my writing and thinking about higher education, the place of the liberal arts, and my role as a teacher and administrator became clearer to me.

In many of the colleges at which I interviewed, faculty members expressed concern that their college's roots in the liberal arts had decayed beyond revival. Other colleges, either Catholic or loosely Christian, wanted to know what I, as an administrator, might do to help foster a renewal of their school's original Christian mission.

At the time, the late 1990s and well into the 2000s, these were the concerns of many small mission-driven schools—places that had begun as teacher institutes or seminaries or strictly liberal arts schools, but which had evolved into colleges that offered programs in business or allied health or other professional areas. I noted that the liberal arts were foundational to all the disciplines and professions. I often argued that if the schools could somehow give students the sense that they were more than consumers, that they were in fact connected to something larger than themselves, then perhaps that was "a good start."

I believe that one way liberal arts informs individuals is by helping a student find his/her place in the miasma of the world, even if that place may be shaky, and to welcome the continual shift from one place to another.

What I began to tell, I now see, is some of the story I now write. Of how I started out in the sciences because I thought they could provide solid answers to the muddled self I had begun to discover. Of how at St. Ben I experienced conversion, that the world I was accustomed to seeing in terms of measurement, the world of mathematical and scientific formulae, could not tell my story. Of how I eschewed a measurable and calculable view of self, and turned toward a view far more mysterious, told through poetry, art, music, philosophy, and novels.

I told of how I thought I had become the "strange bird" of my family. That an unnamed uncle (Uncle Ed) called me the "religious fanatic," and that if I kept reading all that "philosophy and such" I wouldn't be able to talk to anyone. That an unnamed brother-in-law (Jim, Polly's husband), had told me that the liberal arts could lead to "oddness" and that once I headed down that road, it would be hard to come back.

More than anything, more than the doubts (which were many), the gentle putdowns by uncles or brothers-in-law, more than the disruptions (and because of them), the liberal arts had opened in me a deep sense of longing, and that longing had led to a renewed sense of life as a pilgrimage, a journey.

I still believe education can and should provide a sense of liberation and that the liberal arts can foster it—liberation from facile views of "person," from searing oppression, from ubiquitous prejudice, from excessive certainty or sentimentality, from the idols of "success" and "winning." The liberal arts can liberate. In its root, education means "leading forth," from the Latin *educere*.

Where does it lead?

It leads to a broader view of person for one thing. The narrow view of person, for example, what could be called *"homo economicus,"* gives way to a view of person on a journey, what Walker Percy, following Gabriel Marcel, calls *"homo viator,"* person as wayfarer, pilgrim—always on the road, a place between destinations. Such a journey deepens "respect for what we are" (what the Christian tradition calls "an image of God"). The "leading forth" of education fosters desire through longing, not away from the messiness of self and world, but toward them, between the boundaries that family, politics, culture, even church, may create.

A person on such a journey relies on a humble recognition that the individual is lead forth by others, the many writers and thinkers, the poets and musicians and scientists, who came before. Education conserves their works, looks at them afresh, and provides an opening to the liberation they proffer.

Elizabeth Shatswell, a student who pursued a college degree while in prison, states the power of education succinctly:

> The world gets bigger. I didn't understand the Atlantic Ocean was as big as it was, or that people in other countries do things differently. And a program being student-centered and not behavior-centered allows behavior to change. Humanization equates to change. (*The Seattle Times*, August 2, 2024.)

Education leads to a bigger world and can provide an easing of the boundaries, the narrowness and "prison" of thoughts or behaviors. Treating prisoners as educable humans (and not simply as numbers) leads to a "humanization [that equals] change." Shatswell passed into a larger world even while inside physical prison. What are the metaphorical prisons—the hardened boundaries—that keep others locked out of, incapable of experiencing, such humanization and change?

Recollections on a Road Between

Shatswell's experience suggests that education teaches, or should teach, that a prisoner or a street cleaner in Abu Dhabi carries the title "person" no less than Elon Musk—that the street cleaner *is* no less unique than Musk. Although much of education rightly concerns jobs and economic well-being, education is fundamentally about person and self—its ineffable dignity, fragility, and interstitial mystery.

Education can remind us that waypoints are not vantages of certainty, that complexities of self and other and consciousness, of even the cells and proteins that comprise persons, are provisional and beyond ultimate understanding, and when those cells and proteins return to ash or dust, perhaps a new world begins again.

In short, my career in higher education, the difficulties I experienced (many self-inflicted), the joys I had too, the many interviews, the writing I did for talks or for scholarly publication, the little pieces I wrote for newspapers or student organizations, honed my views about the power of the liberal arts. Through story, art, music, philosophy, history, the liberal arts offer another way of knowing, of placing a self nowhere—now, here—on a journey between an ever-receding but "re-collectable" past and a largely unknown future.

Perhaps it is another form of vanity, as Ecclesiastes reminds us, but I think such a "between" understanding of self acknowledges possibility while creating, not simply a "chase after the wind," but openness to a spirit of longing.

───

I return time and again to my initial years of seminary life, where I first experienced the power of education and the transformation, the conversion in thinking it offered me. Those years have been deepened by graduate education, marriage, raising children, and a sometimes joyful, sometimes rocky career. The thrill of finding a new way of seeing things, exploring subjects deeply, shaping the trajectory of institutions and the students who attend them, all these shaped me in ways known and unknown, and they allowed me to see my wayfaring as being between the spaces of hardened boundaries.

I cannot say that I have not been disappointed in or doubted the institutions that have helped to form me—the church has its history of sexual abuse coupled with an often triumphal attitude, both arising from an ugly clericalism. Many educational institutions have devolved into places of quarrelsome dogmatism instead of places of open discourse and discovery. It is understandable that many people have lost faith in both the church and higher education. I am grateful for their shaping me more than I am disappointed in their failings. I remain hopeful in their power to make the world a bigger place.

I think the poem that follows, which I wrote in 2014, captures this sense of hopeful possibility while at the same time acknowledging unsavory history. It opens a space between dismissal and blind faith.

Toward What End?

It's an old story—
warped and maimed
by its messengers
who can be, let's say,
less than savory.

What if it were true after all?

After war in the name of peace,
power disguised as poverty—
triumphantly worn—
or the aching betrayal
of the little ones.

But what if it were true after all?

The blind might see and the lame might walk.
Hearts burning for something—
nearly anything but the sameness—
might find solace in a simple meal,
in a blade of grass.

With thanks to Roberto Bonazzi

11

How long, LORD? Will you utterly forget me?…How long must I carry sorrow in my soul?

—Psalm 13, v 2, 3

As you know by now, Jan and I started our family while I was in grad school, moved them several times around the Covington/Mandeville, Louisiana area, then to New Orleans; to Billings, Montana; to Savannah, Georgia; and finally to San Antonio, Texas. For our family, pilgrimage was not simply an idea.

Jan worked in and out of higher education after we left St. Ben. In New Orleans, she taught part-time and developed a small business as a freelance writer, and in Montana, she volunteered as head of the local Opera Company and also developed local television ads. She directed the ESL program at Savannah College of Art and Design, where I served as Graduate Dean, and when we moved to San Antonio, she worked with the Defense Language Institute (DLI), a training wing of the Air Force, which trains members of US military allies in basic, advanced, and specialized English.

In 2013, Jan was selected for a Mobile Teacher Training program (MTT) in Timor l'Este. The opportunity to travel to far-flung countries stood out as an attraction of her position at DLI. She left for for what was supposed to be a six-month stint. During her first month, she sent emails describing her temporary home, the extreme poverty that surrounded her, an expat jogging group she joined, the local Catholic Church, and the rugged tropical beauty of the island. About five weeks after her arrival, she became worried about a lump on her neck. The lump had appeared not long after she got there, but she attributed it to a cold, brought on by the stress of the long travel.

When the lump did not go away, but in fact grew, she went to see the embassy doctor. The doctor told her they would watch it for another week, but if it were still there, she would need to have it diagnosed in Singapore. It continued to grow, so Jan went to a hospital in Singapore. At about three in the morning one night, I received a call from her. Groggy from sleep, I heard Jan's distressed voice. "Eddie," she said while crying, "I have cancer!" I blanched, and whatever cobwebs I had cleared immediately. "Oh, no," I said. "I am sorry." Tears still flowing, she told me she had been diagnosed in Singapore with cancer of the tonsils. She would be coming home on the first available flight, not even returning to Timor to get her belongings.

My mind whirled. *Cancer!* That was something that happened to other people! I was scared—for Jan, for us, for the life we had built over the years. I could not imagine Jan's fear. In a country halfway around the world, no one there with her, and receiving such horrid news!

While Jan worked with DLI to arrange an emergency flight home, I tried to do what I could to get things in place so she could begin treatment as soon as she arrived.

I contacted my brother Mike, who put me in touch with a good friend at Ochsner in New Orleans, who, incidentally, had treated John's ears when he was a baby. That fellow put me in touch with an ENT surgeon in San Antonio. I wrote him and he responded immediately. A friend put me in touch with a cancer specialist in San Antonio. I spoke to his nurse, and she suggested we plan a visit after surgery. All this while Jan awaited a flight home.

When she did arrive, we held each other close and had long talks about what directions we might take. Should she have surgery? Do we like the doctor? What other steps might we take? Why did this happen at all?

By now you understand that writing is a way for me to cope, to come to terms, not only with myself, but with whatever "slings and arrows outrageous fortune" might cast my way. So, I wrote the poem that follows soon after we learned of Jan's diagnosis:

Recollections on a Road Between

Beginnings

"And so it begins,"
we said, pulling out the drive
and onto the street
as we had done thousands
of times before. On the way—
the first appointment.
And then we said it
again en route to
fated surgery.

Where does it begin—
I want to ask—this moment
like any other
preceded and ceded
to several more, like a
place in line? Where or
when can you say that
anything begins?

If you start with the
lump, you know it came from the
mass in the tonsil.
But start there, and you
know that growth has a distant
genesis—a time
and place of its own.

You could be extreme
and go back to your birth, but
even then you are foiled,
for despite thinking
contrarily, you are not
your own beginning.

Can you say, then, that
a design from the launch of
time has planted this
in you? It affronts to
say so, to suggest that a
will or force would plan
such a thing, that it
is something more than accident
or chance encounter.

That it starts, you can
have no doubt—a certainty
that belies weary
intellectualism—
there like no other
thing in a space—and
still seeking a source.

༄

She had the surgery within a week of her return. It was successful, except that in removing a group of cancer-fill lymph nodes, the surgeon stretched a nerve that controls movement of the right shoulder.

Soon after, we met with the cancer specialist, but we left feeling worse. He wanted, he said, "to throw the kitchen sink" of radiation and then chemo-therapy at her, especially the latter. We liked the ENT surgeon very much, and wanted his opinion about treatment after surgery. He was hesitant to go against the recommendation of the cancer specialist, but we could tell he might have had different thoughts about the course of treatment. I had read that in some cases like Jan's, neither surgery, nor extensive chemo was needed. I found the name of another ENT cancer specialist at MD Anderson. He also responded immediately to my email and suggested we travel to Houston for a consult with him and a radiation oncologist. We did.

When we saw the professionalism of MD Anderson staff (even the housekeepers in the hallways asked how they might help us), the holistic approach they employed, and the extreme competency and empathy of the physicians and nurses, we knew this was the place we wanted. The radiation oncologist, for example, told us he would not have recommended surgery, but that since that route had already been taken, he would do everything he could to minimize the side-effects of radiation. Chemo would not be the "kitchen sink" but targeted doses to kill whatever cancer cells might remain.

Jerrie and Don graciously offered a large upstairs room at their home as Jan's home away from home. We set up a series of "nurses" (Jan's friends) who came during the weeks of treatment to drive her to and from appointments and keep her company. At home for summer break, John was with her for the first couple of weeks, but as treatments went on and the effects of radiation set in, Jan grew weaker, and the friends flew in.

On Thursdays or Fridays, I drove to Houston after work, spent the weekend with Jan or took her back home, picked up the next "nurse," got her set up at Jerrie's place, then returned to San Antonio. The Department of Defense has a "borrowed leave" program such that folks with excess annual leave can "donate" that leave to people like Jan, who needed extended leave for serious illness. This remarkable program allowed Jan the time to receive treatment in Houston, away from our home.

We had been told by the radiation oncologist's nurse that the treatment could be "rough." He wasn't kidding. The skin on Jan's neck blistered and oozed. She swallowed with great difficulty and pain, and she lost her appetite and taste, a true misery for someone who appreciates good food. Her saliva glands, fried by the radiation, quit working, which made problems not only for eating but for her teeth as well. Many patients need to have feeding tubes to maintain nutrition and weight. Jan was determined NOT to have a tube, so often drank "The Hulk," a 2000-calorie concoction from Smoothie King. To this day she cannot tolerate smoothies.

I wrote another poem:

This Time of Sickness

This time of sickness
has been a time out of time
intense yet blurry
fathomless and stark.

Recollections on a Road Between

Like psalmists of old
you wonder, "How long, O Lord?"
First the shock, then the
fear, followed by a

routine like Lauds or
Vespers. Your "good veins"—so the
nurses said—infused
with poison tonic.

And then the burn of
invisible rays, no flash,
a silent power,
unseen, gradual

whose end—hoped for and
unknown—brings weakness and doubt,
weeks of discipline,
involuntary

fast, a tasteless joke
made at the expense of you
who love to cook and
savor all things made.

And still the struggles
persist, a problem hearing,
unsavory dreams,
restless vigils mark

a time whose end seems
further with each crossed signpost—
watching and waiting.
for the healing day.

Part of the team at MD Anderson included not only a dentist, but a speech therapist, not because Jan lost her speech, but because she needed to strengthen the muscles that controlled swallowing and neck and jaw movement. She had a series of exercises that I and her nurses practiced with her several times daily. When the final day of radiation arrived, she rang the bell in celebration (a tradition), knowing, however, that the effects of those final doses would linger into the coming weeks. Because she would be in bad shape, we asked Kelley, her brother David's wife and a nurse practitioner, to serve as her final volunteer care taker.

We continued the neck and jaw exercises for several weeks and months after Kelly left. Jan found a good dentist in San Antonio, someone familiar with radiation patients. She was faithful about prescribed daily fluoride treatments, self-administered each night, and slowly regained her strength and appetite.

One night about two weeks after Kelly left, I was awakened by a thud. "What happened?" I asked half asleep. "I fell," Jan said.

She had fallen because she had passed out from anemia. And she had nasty gash from having hit her head on the bed frame. I drove her to the hospital right behind our house, where they cleaned up the wound and stapled her scalp. They wanted to keep her longer for observation. We explained her condition, that she had just been released from MD Anderson, and that we lived literally two blocks from the ER. Tired of hospitals, we just wanted to be home. We promised to be right back if things took a turn for the worse. Amazingly, grudgingly, they agreed.

Jan's taste did not return for a while, but it did return. She still uses tablets to help with saliva production. And she had physical therapy for the shoulder damage, which lingers but has markedly improved. Her stamina, her hard work during treatment, her determination, coupled with the targeted, holistic approach offered by MD Anderson, assured that lingering side effects would be minimized or disappear entirely.

Although we will never forget that she had cancer, she has been cancer free many years, and her recovery is complete. We joke that she will die of something other than tonsillar cancer.

She was selected for an MTT to Cairo, at which I joined her for two weeks, a wonderful time of discovery for both of us. A year after she returned from Cairo, she was chosen for a long-term assignment to Abu Dhabi.

That posting allowed me to retire from my work in higher education, and among many other things, begin to write the early drafts of the story you now read.

12

Here in the desert I had found all that I asked; I knew that should never find it again.
—Wilfrid Thesiger, *Arabian Sands*

Jan and I arrived in Abu Dhabi late in the night of June 26, 2018. May and the early part of June had been a whirlwind—of closing on the sale of our house and selling our cars, of saying goodbye to friends and family, of learning the processes of a government-funded move and interminable acronyms: UAB (unaccompanied baggage); HHG (household goods); JTR (joint travel regulations), CONUS (Continental United States), OCONUS (Outside Continental United States), POV (Personally Owned Vehicle), and many others.

Although we had begun anew in so many places, this move held a special character. I would be retired, Jan would be working, and the kids would be more or less on their own. Ben and Shannon worked in Seattle. Madeleine and James, married in 2017, treated themselves to a six-month jaunt around a good part of the world (Japan, Singapore, Thailand, India, Abu Dhabi, Turkey, Greece, Abu Dhabi again, Italy) to celebrate Madeleine completing her PhD. John worked on a Master's in Physics at UNC-Chapel Hill, while his soon-to-be spouse, Lindsey, worked on a Master's in Public Administration. They were married in 2019.

In Abu Dhabi, we had obligations only to Jan's work, to our new roles as parents of adults, and to the usual responsibilities of being human. Our expenses were limited to food and entertainment. While this new phase carried some fear and trembling, those qualms were overshadowed by the excitement of living as expats in a well-developed Middle Eastern country.

Although we had seen floor plans of our apartment online, when we saw our new home in person, we were astonished at the size—four bedrooms, four and a half baths, a large kitchen, a laundry room (which would have served as the "maid's quarters" in earlier times), and a large living room/dining room that opened onto a balcony looking out to an inlet of the Arabian Gulf, the Etihad Towers, the Emirates Palace Hotel, the ADNOC building, and the new Presidential Palace complex. The apartment, we agreed, provided an unaccustomed luxury. Even after midnight, the city throbbed with activity.

Like newlyweds, Jan and I looked out from the balcony toward toward the Emirates Palace Hotel, the Etihad Towers, and toward an unknown future, and we nearly giggled at our good fortune.

Jan standing on the balcony of our apartment in Abu Dhabi on the night of our arrival. June 26, 2018.

⤸

We were expats. Since my time in Rome, the expat life had appealed to me. I liked this between existence, from the US, but not living in the US. It gave me, like Percy's wounded man in the battle, a fresh view of "home," a different view of myself in relation to home. Jan drove an hour each way out to the desert, where she taught at Zayed Military City. I wrote poetry and essays, walked or rode the bicycle along the Corniche, played golf, and enjoyed encountering folks from all parts of the world.

After settling in for a few months, I began working part-time at the US embassy, doing everything from answering the phone, to helping out in human resources, to serving as a security escort and working in the economic section. We took a road trip to Oman in August, visited the Grand Mosque in Muscat, discovered mandi, a rice and meat dish much like Indian biryani, but with slightly different spices. In the fall we took a trip to Paris and Bordeaux, to meet one of the Roman Ladies, Beth, and her husband John. Madeleine and James visited after a six-week stay in India, and in December they came back along with Ben and Shannon and John and Lindsey. A family reunion in Abu Dhabi!

Visiting the Sheik Zayed Grand Mosque in Abu Dhabi as a family. Women are required to cover their heads and wear conservative garb while visiting the mosque. December, 2018. (l to r) Me, James (Madeleine's spouse), Benjamin, John, Shannon (Ben's spouse) Jan, Madeleine, Lindsey (John's spouse). December, 2018.

Our kids and their spouses in Abu Dhabi at a marina behind the Etihad Towers (background left) and the ADNOC building (background right). (l to r) John, Lindsey, Madeleine, James, Shannon, and Ben. December, 2018.

In June of 2019, we traveled to Leipzig, Germany, to meet Fr. Sean Duggan, OSB, who had played piano at our wedding reception and who was part of the program for the International Bach Festival. Still later in the summer travelled to Sydney, Australia, for a week and from there up to Cairns for two weeks, where we hiked, explored the high plains of Australia and took a boat out to the Great Barrier Reef.

In fall of 2019, I applied to be what was called the "Staff Assistant" in the Ambassador's office, and for a year worked full-time as a member of the state department, ensuring that the flow of cables, decision memos, briefing memos, and other "paper" kept moving. I had never stepped foot in an embassy before, and here I was in the pulse of this one in Abu Dhabi. I counted myself lucky to be among the hardworking diplomats who do most of their work anonymously, eyes and ears on the ground with their host-country counterparts to help fashion diplomatic partnerships.

While I may not have agreed with the policies of the administration at the time, I practiced discretion, like the frontline diplomats and military personnel who had worked for various administrations with little regard for whatever their political sensibilities might have been.

Reminiscent of my years working in higher ed, I witnessed political squabbles within the ranks of embassy personnel. Since I was no longer on a career track, however, I felt free to do my job without worrying too much about them.

I couldn't help but be aware of the millions of migrant laborers, who had left Pakistan, India, Sri Lanka, the Philippines, Uganda, and many other countries to try to find a living wage in this small, wealthy nation, a wage their home countries could not supply. A hundred or so had found employment in the embassy, where they could garner better wages than many of their fellow countrymen who worked in construction or maintenance or the many malls around the city. I felt connected to them and their plight, even though my life was and is very different from theirs.

⁓

Back in 2010, when I served as Graduate Dean at Savannah College of Art and Design (SCAD), I was sent to Dubai on a recruitment junket with several students and the director of the SCAD museum, who was participating in Art Dubai. We were in the UAE for only six days, one of which included an excursion to Abu Dhabi.

My small group of SCAD compatriots and I stopped at Saadiyat Island on our way into the city. There, we were treated to a scale model of the entire island, which was to house, along with beach fronts and a marina, the cultural center of Abu Dhabi—with sites for the Louvre, which was already under construction, the Guggenheim Abu Dhabi, still awaiting construction today, and Zayed National Museum. Models of the museums looked like something out of a sci-fi film—wonderfully futuristic, tantalizing. How could I have known that about eight years later, I'd become an expat in Abu Dhabi?

When I read about the Louvre Abu Dahbi's opening in November of 2017, Jan had already received the news that she'd be posted in Abu Dhabi. The Louvre was high on our visit list. After we arrived, a friend told us that Friday mornings were the best time to see the Louvre, so we took her advice.

On the morning we decided to go, I went to fill up the car at the ADNOC station across the street from our apartment building and thought I'd surprise Jan with a Chicken Sausage Egg McMuffin, available at the McDonald's in the station's mini-mart. The Louvre and McDonald's! A baguette and café au lait would have been more appropriate, of course.

Only a short trip from our apartment on the Corniche to Saadiyat Island, the drive to the Louvre Abu Dhabi took about twenty minutes. We arrived just around opening time—10:00 a.m.

The July sun was already bearing down on the entryway, a concrete lattice-work that offers welcomed, if spotty, shade. As with most public spaces in Abu Dhabi, the grounds were meticulously maintained, cleaned, and watered, so that green Bermuda grass contrasted with the museum's white walls and pewter dome. The structure stood out from and accentuated the azure hues of the Arabian Gulf.

Greeted by friendly South Asian staff, we found our way to the ticket office and joined as members so that we could return as often as we liked. Membership not only included the usual perks—member previews, priority access, i.e., no waiting in line, discounts at the café and gift shop—but also membership in the Paris Louvre, the Musee d'Orsay, and the Centre Georges Pompidou. We started to plan a trip back to Paris even as we paid the membership fee.

The collection is divided into twelve galleries, arranged chronologically and globally, so that the gallery on ancient civilization, for example, includes pieces from Egypt, China, and India. This pattern repeats itself. The gallery on religion includes works dedicated not only to Islam, but to Judaism, Hinduism, Buddhism, and Christianity. It's a bold and welcomed ecumenical stance. I was particularly struck by a bronze of the Dancing Shiva from Tamil Nadu.

As we moved from gallery to gallery, we looked through windows open to the domed exterior spaces and water, teasing us with the play of light and shadow in both. Jean Nouvel, the architect, surely planned it so, knowing that art is fundamentally a play of light and shadow, texture and color and shape. Here, architecture was also art.

We lingered at some galleries and went through others more quickly. We spent a lot of time in the one on religion. The gallery on impressionism highlighted the movement's forbears and heirs, presented in the context of rapid industrialization and the travel that it facilitated. We found the collection neither vast nor fatiguing, but rather small, well-structured, and smartly exhibited in spacious, yet not overwhelming, rooms.

We were eager to go outside under the dome, which we had seen only in fragments from the inside. Once outside, the genius of the design became more apparent and exciting.

Nouvel said he wanted the dome to cover a city, not only of art, which it surely does, but also a traditional Arabic city, with its white walls and rectangular blocks dappled under the palm-frond-like patterns created by the dome. In some quarters, steps take you down to the water's edge, like a beachfront, while others provide vistas of open water and the gleaming city beyond. Still others open into an oasis-like pool. Each turn around a corner revealed a new vista, and sometimes a gust of wind.

The central part of Giuseppe Penone's *Germination* stands starkly (yet alluringly) near the "city's" center.

In the "city's" center (under the dome) at the Louvre Abu Dhabi, with Giuseppe Penone's *Germination*. July, 2018.

This space lifted our spirits, as though Nouvel hit upon the secret of perpetual motion, with its shifting light and rippling waters, moving with the visitor, with the tides, and with the arcing sun or moon. "One cannot step in the same stream twice," said Heraclitus long ago. The same, it could be said, of the Louvre Abu Dhabi.

When we got back to our apartment, I looked up more articles about the Louvre, Giuseppe Penone, and Jean Nouvel. As with most construction projects in the Gulf Region, the Louvre and its magnificent dome casts other, darker, shadows.

Before coming to Abu Dhabi, Jan and I researched our new home. We read stories of the UAE's influence peddling in the 2016 presidential election, its participation in the Yemini civil war, its stultifying summer heat, and its track record regarding migrant workers. When I Googled "Louvre Abu Dhabi," a link to an article about the contentious labor practices involved during its construction popped up. Not only was the selling of the Louvre "brand" a sticking point for many, but the use of a migrant labor force prompted 120 international artists to urge a boycott of the Louvre Abu Dhabl altogether.

Nevertheless, I was curious to know more about the plight of the migrant workers, those who maintained the beautiful Corniche, those who worked in every retail center, and those who built the spectacular Louvre.

It's easy for Westerners to feel superior to the Emiratis when it comes to labor. Americans in particular, with our myth of exceptionalism, think we have the best of everything—best healthcare, best standard of living, best "values." We often let our naive indignity and arrogance (my own included) brand other countries as not measuring up. A friend back home, for example, spoke of the hypocrisy of the Emiratis, who profess a peaceful vision of Islam, who are called to prayer five times daily, yet who exploit their workforce.

While the UAE and members of the Gulf Cooperation Council import their workers at levels far beyond most economies (somewhere around 88 percent of the UAE's population are migrants) and while 99.9 percent of these migrants will never become UAE citizens, Europe and the United States also display the complexities associated with offering humane treatment to those fleeing their home countries—seeking a better place, more money to send home to their families, and a chance at bettering their plight.

In 2021, migrant workers from the UAE sent a collective 47 billion dollars to their home countries. It's an astonishing amount, made more so when you consider that most migrant workers earn salaries less than $500 per month. Unable to find work in their home countries, they come to the Gulf region in hopes of finding (and funding) a better life for their families "back home."

Abuses do exist, however. In our own apartment, for example, Jan and I were shocked to discover that what we use as the laundry room, a windowless space about 8 by 15 feet, is called the "maid's room." A person would have actually lived there. When we expressed our dismay to a South Asian Indian whose job it was to orient us to our new home, he said wryly, "Welcome to the UAE." While organizations such as Human Rights Watch, Amnesty International, and Migrant Rights perform noble service to the cause of improving workers' rights and making real change, abuse still occurs.

Opportunities exist as well, however, opportunities unavailable in workers' home countries, which is why they migrate in the first place—to fulfill the human desire of finding a way to support themselves, their families, and hoping that their children will have a better life than theirs.

We should work to correct wrongs. Overturning slavery and the Jim Crow South by war, activism, and legislation was the right thing to do, but elements of its legacy exist in fact if not in the ideal of law. These elements can and should be rooted out. Certainly, we should call out injustice, work for the common good, and protect the rights of the defenseless. These wrongs exist and persist because we are ourselves flawed beings and build institutions and structures that are fallible.

I think again of the gallery dedicated to the world's religions and the tenth century bronze statue of the dancing Shiva from Tamil Nadu. He holds in two of his hands the drum of creation and the fire of destruction, his third hand is set in a posture of protection, while the fourth beckons viewers to worship. He stands on one leg, which also suppresses ignorance, while his other leg displays grace and balance. His asymmetric limbs evoke at once terror and joy, balance and imbalance. An image of the world—creator-destroyer, filled with tremendous beauty and horrendous wrongs—he reminds us that we participate in both. Our action (or inaction) creates and destroys.

The Shiva points to our interstitial existence—between terror and joy, knowledge and ignorance, beauty and exploitation, beauty built on the backs of migrant workers.

Legislation, social programs, and boycotts can mitigate the effects of structural and social wrongs, but history shows that they won't eradiate them. The Louvre Abu Dhabi, like the foundations of American democracy, may have been built on wrongs committed against fellow human beings. That fact, however, should mute neither the continued cry for justice nor the quest for, and experience of, beauty.

⁓

In September of 2018, Madeleine and her husband James joined us in Abu Dhabi. Having spent six weeks in India, they needed some pampering, cleanliness, and rest, all of which we happily offered. We took them to the sites we had come to know—the Grand Mosque, the Louvre, the malls. Madeleine and James told stories of their experiences in India and the other places they had visited so far. We had excited conversations of place and home, what they mean, how travel (or living as an expat) offers a fresher view of both home and place.

With them, we drove out to the Liwa Oasis, about two hours away and part of the famed Rub al Khali (the "Empty Quarter"), a contiguous desert of some 192,000 square miles, encompassing parts not only of the UAE, but also Saudi Arabia, Oman, and Yemen. Hauntingly beautiful, the sand forms majestic dunes in hues of red, peach, and ocre, hues that, like the dunes themselves, shifted in color depending on the time of day. It may be called the "Empty Quarter," but its vastness exhilarated me. It was, in a sense, a place that is no place, nowhere, empty, but also full!

Wilfred Thesiger, the famed British explorer, had traversed the Empty Quarter twice and recounted his story of those crossings in his classic *Arabian Sands*. I read it even before Jan and I left San Antonio to live in Abu Dhabi and was eager to see the desert he loved.

Early in their visit, James said excitedly, "This has got to be the most diverse place I've ever seen." He was referring, of course, to the millions of migrant workers who hail from all reaches of the world—Pakistan, India, Nepal, Uganda, Cameroon, Nigeria, Ghana, Sudan, South Africa, Namibia, Syria, Lebanon, Egypt, Somalia, England, Ireland, Germany, France, Serbia, Croatia, Romania, Australia, New Zealand, Russia, Ukraine, Malaysia, The Philippines, China, Korea, and of course, the United States. We couldn't argue about that. Toward the end of their stay, Madeleine noted with equal vigor that Abu Dhabi didn't feel that foreign to her, certainly not like India had. I thought both of their statements were true.

Except for the extreme summer heat and humidity, Abu Dhabi didn't seem like a desert city. The magnificent Etihad Towers, visible from our kitchen window, point to an unparalleled present prosperity and hope of an equally glistening future. Not only the skyline makes Abu Dhabi seem un-desert-like, but also its cleanliness and order—well maintained streets, the beautiful Corniche, which combines the stunning blue water of the Arabian Gulf, clean beaches, boardwalks and sidewalks meandering through a landscape dotted with date palms, acacia, and Bermuda grass, food huts that provide everything from crepes to biryani, ice cream to luqaimats, and events such as firework displays, music concerts, air races—even dhow (traditional Arab boat) races—conspire to make one forget that Abu Dhabi had ever been anything but a thriving city.

Thus I was surprised that in his preface to the 1984 reprint of *Arabian Sands*, Wilfred Thesiger called Abu Dhabi an "Arabian Nightmare." His crossings of the Empty Quarter with Bedu guides had brought him a freedom unattainable in his modern world. Toward the end of his classic story, he writes:

> Here in the desert I had found all that I asked; I knew that should never find it again. But it was not only this personal sorrow that distressed me. I realized that the Bedu with whom I had lived and travelled, and in whose company I had found contentment, were doomed. Some people maintain that they will be better off when they have exchanged the hardship and poverty of the desert for the security of a materialistic world. This I do not believe.

Thesiger reminded his readers, again in the 1984 preface, that "the changes which occurred in the space of a decade or two were as great as those which occurred in Britain between the early Middle Ages and the present day." The life of the Bedu, while heralded as the tradition of the Emiratis, is hardly present today, so Thesiger's dire prophecy seems in part to have come true.

Anyone who might like a view of this whiplash of time need only look at photographs of a young Abu Dhabi from Thesiger's collection at the Jahili Fort in Al Ain or from Edward Henderson's collection in his *Arabian Destiny*. In the lobby of Hilton, the first hotel built (in 1968) along Abu Dhabi's beachfront, a photograph of the new hotel shows it promisingly stark, alone on the sand. The hotel's exterior remains largely the same as it was upon completion.

We took James and Madeleine out to the Liwa Oasis. During our drive, we experienced some of what Thesiger might have seen on his crossings—vast, empty expanses, multi-hued sands of cinnamon, peach, and tan, extraordinary dunes providing texture and contour to the emptiness. Though the road was well built, sand drifts reminded us that a road was probably not intended in this beautiful space.

We wanted to see the Moreeb Dune, heralded as the highest dune in the world. At the end of the road, upon our arrival, we were disappointed. We saw the dune, but we also found, at its foot, a sports center—complete with stadium, lights, parking lots, and children's play areas. The center is devoted to dune climbing—the motorized variety—during the Moreeb Dune Festival. I suppose if one wants to climb dunes in this way, one should do so on the tallest in the world. And yet, the presence of the sports facility provided an abrupt disjunction to the surrounding beauty and to the Moreeb Dune itself. Jan said, "If this had been developed in the United States, folks would have protested loudly."

The development at Moreeb Dune offers a stark reminder that place, the experience of place, is formed by culture, yet another reason for travel or for living in unfamiliar places.

I admit I have something of a theologically-hued, romantic, vision of the desert. My attraction to it is colored by biblical accounts of the Israelites wandering, of Jesus confronting temptation (and Dostoevsky's magisterial reflection on this in his famous "Grand Inquisitor" chapter), of John the Baptist, of the early church's "desert fathers," of St. Anthony's Coptic Monastery in Egypt, of Thomas Merton in his hermitage, of Binx Bolling reading T.E. Lawrence in Walker Percy's *The Moviegoer*. The desert is an interstitial place if ever there was one—between, there, but seemingly nowhere, apparently without history (or hiding it), a sort of an ocean, eternally present, ever changing.

The desert, a place of solitude, might allow one the chance to confront one's demons and thus find freedom from them. Thesiger sought (and found) freedom during his arduous crossings. His passages colored my expectation, and eventual disappointment. I had hoped to see nothing but Moreeb Dune, perhaps only with an identifying plaque, but the sports complex jolted me out of my romantic longings and reminded me that development had reached even this empty space.

Recollections on a Road Between

The first time Thesiger visited Abu Dhabi, it was a city of about two thousand inhabitants. Now it is home to nearly 1.3 million people—and growing. Sheik Zayed bin Sultan al Nahyan, the founder of the UAE, wanted to make the desert green and to provide comfort and stability to his beloved countrymen. Since he founded the country in 1971, his vision has provided not only extraordinarily rapid growth, but also an oasis of calm in the midst of a roiling region.

One questions the sustainability of building metropolises such as Abu Dhabi, Dubai, and Sharjah in this desert peninsula, but it cannot be denied that Sheik Zayed and his successors have provided for their people. Zayed is justifiably beloved as a visionary, a statesman, and a humanitarian, providing not only for his own country but offering opportunity, however stained by exploitation, to diverse multitudes of immigrant workers.

Even amidst the great diversity that James noted, a lack of "foreignness," as Madeleine pointed out, pervades. The abundant consumer options available—from fast food outlets such as Popeye's and McDonalds, Wendy's, Chili's, Subway, and Baskin and Robbins—retail outlets for all buyers, particularly high-end consumers, fill the many magnificent malls that are ubiquitous in Abu Dhabi and Dubai. While the malls give relief from the stultifying heat and humidity of the summer months, rampant consumerism stifles a sense of being in a "different" place.

This sense finds reinforcement from a feeling of sterility that insinuates itself on many who live here. While the government secures a future for its denizens, as any government should, the dependence on migrants to run the economy does not inspire pride. I sometimes asked waiters, cabbies, or store clerks if they liked their work. The response I got most often was a hapless shrug and an acknowledgement that the money they made here was better than what they could get at home. They seemed unconnected to their work, their employers, or to the country—except to say that they felt safe there. They invariably expressed a longing for home.

Thus, a sense of temporariness pervaded the cities. When I visited any mall or "hypermarket," I couldn't help but notice myriad stands of luggage for sale.

The temporary people were not just the lowest echelon of workers, though that group had little opportunity for advancement beyond what they agreed to when they came. This sense also affected professional staff who had only a very narrow path to long-term residency if they wanted it.

Nor did longevity have any bearing on staying there. I often played golf with a Sri Lankan who had worked for Etihad Airways and lived in Abu Dhabi for more than thirty-five years. He had no path to citizenship, tried to go home, but was stranded, first by COVID, then by the collapse of the Sri Lankan economy brought on by government corruption. He purchased an annual visa, at high cost, from visa vendors in Ras al Khaimah, and at the time Jan and I left, he hoped to be able to join his children who had migrated to Canada. He knew he needed to wait, however, in Abu Dhabi, which had become for him a sort of no-man's-land, until his children could sponsor him and his wife in Canada.

Another contributor to this feeling of sterility has to do with the extensive planning that created the UAE. When we lived there, the UAE celebrated what would have been Sheik Zayed's 100th birthday. A photo of Sheik Zayed crouched over a model of the city with Dr. Abdulrahman Makhlouf could be found in various places around the city. No one can build a country without planning, of course, yet there was (and is) a sense that the UAE had been overplanned. The cleanliness, the futuristic architecture (which is quite beautiful!), the emphasis on glitz, the whiplash of time, and the appearance of perfection superseded organic growth.

While the architecture, the roads, the consumer amenities were (and are) dazzling, they feel soul-less. Dubai spent millions of dirhams to recreate its "old city" along the Creek. When I visited it, however, I didn't catch a whiff of age, as one might walking through the French Quarter in New Orleans, the Khan al Khalili in Cairo, or the Latin Quarter in Paris. Instead I felt a bit like I was walking through "Yesteryear" at a theme park. I heard many people say, in fact, that Dubai and Abu Dhabi "felt something like Disneyland."

In Walker Percy's *The Moviegoer*, Binx Bolling speaks of the "genie-soul" of a place, what he calls the "the sense of the place, the savor…of the place which every place has or else is not a place…. There it is as big as life, the genie-soul of the place which, wherever you go, you must meet and master first thing or be met and mastered."

Though the tourist shops in the UAE were full of genie lamps, one was hard-pressed to find Percy's "genie-soul" in its cities.

I grant that the UAE's cities are still young, so perhaps it is unfair to compare them to storied cities of the world. The vast, formless desert is the UAE's past, and that "no-place" captures its soul. The UAE tries to manufacture a soul in the cities, but the soul of a place can't be fabricated.

Recollections on a Road Between

Was it my Western, American prejudice that prevented my feeling a sense of place? Europeans scoff at Americans and their scant sense of place and history, often true enough. Henry Ford, the secular saint of American industrialism, famously called history "bunk." Ralph Waldo Emerson saw the American experience as an opportunity to create a "new man," with a new vision, in a new place, unfettered by the shackles of history. Is the UAE following the USA with its presumed lack of history and sense of place?

In 1991, in the preface to yet another reprint of *Arabian Sands*, Thesiger recanted his dour outlook for the UAE:

> I visited Abu Dhabi…in 1990 for an exhibition of my photographs…. On this occasion I found myself reconciled to the inevitable changes which have occurred in the Arabia of today and are typified by the United Arab Emirates. Abu Dhabi is now an impressive modern city, made pleasant in this barren land by avenues of trees and green lawns.

While he says he has changed his mind, Thesiger's tone is hardly enthusiastic. It betrays shades of elegy—"inevitable changes," "impressive modern city," "made pleasant." The UAE's glistening cities reflect the inexorability of history, and even Thesiger offers his grudging praise.

But his elegiac tone counters the soulful narrative of his desert crossings and my own attraction to the vast betweenness of the Empty Quarter. Thesiger's tone made me wonder: If the soul of the desert didn't reside in the "impressive modern city" in 1991, and if I didn't find it there in 2022, will it have found residence there 250 years hence?

13

Some days in late August at home are like this, the air thin and eager like this, with something in it sad and nostalgic and familiar.

–William Faulkner, *The Sound and the Fury*

Jan's assignment ended in June 2022. After four years in Abu Dhabi, we had to return to San Antonio.

In the months leading to our departure, the news from our homeland wasn't encouraging: a mass shooting at a school in Uvalde, Texas; political divisions more unbridgeable than ever; the legitimacy of the Biden administration was being questioned; the specter of COVID and its impact on the economy and supply chains loomed; the idea of shared truth seemed out of reach; and anger seemed to define the national mood.

Was this home?

During our time in Abu Dhabi, our kids and their spouses had migrated to Washington State. Ben and Shannon had a beautiful baby girl in 2020 (at the height of COVID) and they lived in West Seattle. Madeleine had taken a job at a community college in southeast Washington, but longed to move west of the Cascades, which she and James did soon after Jan and I returned. They now live in Mt. Vernon. John and Lindsey also moved, first to Tumwater and then to Puyallop, but they bought a house in Olympia not long after we returned to the US.

I began this story of myself with questions about home: What is home? What is it like? Does it imply ownership? Can I be "at home" despite disruptions and displacement, that is to say, by "leaving home?"

I have come to see that much of this story of myself centers on home. My many passages—from New Orleans to Lafayette, back to New Orleans, to Saint Ben, to Rome, back to New Orleans, back to Rome, to graduate school, to Covington, then back to New Orleans yet again, then Montana, Savannah, San Antonio, Abu Dhabi and back to San Antonio, and then to Tacoma—all became home.

Having written so much about passages in time and memory, I see the passages that comprise my story as perhaps a longing for "home."

And so I end this autobiography, a story of my life written by myself, with reflections on a trip Jan and I took up to the Pacific Northwest from San Antonio to help Ben, Madeleine, and John settle into their new homes.

∽

The vistas are stunning. The Olympics to the west and the Cascades to the east, blue sky reflected in waters of the sound, houses dotting evergreen-filled hills. The air is crisp, hints of salt water mixed with musk of western hemlock, Douglas fir, red cedar. Mt. Baker and Mt. Rainier stand regally as reminders of roiling powers deep below rich farmland. Blackberries are everywhere (invaders from England) while huckleberries seek what sunlight they can in the loamy soil under the canopies of the fir-laden foothills.

This place will be our new home. What are transplanted southerners, filled with memories of moonlight and magnolias, heat and humidity, the storied, once-defeated, now Sunbelt South, going to make of life in the Pacific Northwest with its cool summers and long, grey winters? Will clipped-vowelled, slightly nasal voices welcome diphthongal languor, folks used to saying hello to passersby?

Our kids began the migration to the PNW (its coy acronym) in the summer of 2023. Jan and I will complete it. We'll be strung along the majestic Puget Sound—Ben, the first to land there, in West Seattle, John in Olympia, Madeleine in Mt. Vernon, and Jan and I in Tacoma, where we purchased, while living in Abu Dhabi during the pandemic, a house just south of the city center. Perhaps the purchase signaled an effort at stability amidst the uncertainty of the time. The house will be our retirement home. The PNW our retirement place.

Retiring and remaining in one place is an odd concept, given that we moved the family, as you've read, quite a bit during our working years. You might consider us among the subjects of Carole King's "So Far Away." Can we, to continue with King's classic, make a place home and stay there?

In West Seattle, we helped Ben with his daughter Rylan while Shannon took a work trip to Alaska. From there we helped John and Lindsey settle in to their home in Olympia, and then went up to Mt. Vernon where Madeleine and James, the newest to settle west of the Cascades, had produced an Excel-spreadsheet-list of tasks for us in their new place. My hands cramped with the unaccustomed fine- and large-muscle-work.

Carole King's song intruded on me as I drilled, sanded, and painted—can I stay in one place? And her question behind that question—what is "home?"—haunts me like the ghosts of memory in Faulkner.

While in Abu Dhabi, Jan and I rubbed shoulders with folks who've made careers in the US Military and the State Department, people whose lives embody deracination—two or three years here, four years there, until a new posting brings a new place to call home. More often than not, when I asked them where they were from back in the States, they told me their parents, also in the military or foreign service, had moved around so much, they had little connection to their place of birth. They had a hard time saying where home was for them.

As I've said, Abu Dhabi is a sort of temporary place for millions of migrant workers seeking a job that will allow them to send money to their families in places as near as Pakistan or as far away as the Philippines. For them, home loomed as a magnet, drawing wistful memories. The difficult conditions under which they toiled offered more opportunity than they could find in their home countries. Still, they wanted more than anything to return home, its remembered attractions—extended family, children, home cooking—despite its acknowledged deficits—lack of jobs, corruption, insecurity.

What is home?

In San Antonio, the neighborhood we lived in was about ninety percent Hispanic, made up of immigrants and the descendants of immigrants from Mexico and Central America. When I went out for morning walks, I passed by a house with a large sign on the front porch that read "Home Sweet Home."

Jan and I returned to San Antonio from Abu Dhabi in late June of 2022. Less than a week after our return, sixty-four immigrants, forty-eight of them dead, were found in and around an abandoned trailer. The lure of a new home is strong. And the numbers of people seeking new homes continues to grow—because of wars (Afghanistan, Yemen, Syria, Sudan, Ukraine), because of drug trafficking, corruption, and crime (Mexico, Central America), and because of climate change.

Today, one reads stories not only of people dying in search of home, but of folks telling Asian Americans and African Americans—people born in the US—to "go home!"

The US is a country founded by immigrants and developed on the importation of slave labor and the violent displacement of indigenous peoples. Here, the concept of home is, at best, fraught. Whose home is this?

When we were in Olympia with John and Lindsey we attended Shakespeare in the park—a lively, well-paced performance of *Twelfth Night* by Animal Fire Theatre. The flyer advertising the event identified the venue as "Squaxin Park (formerly known as Priest Point)." The two names say much about place, displacement, and home, and to emphasize the point, the leader of the troupe took time before the play to remember and acknowledge the park's original inhabitants. In today's fractious political climate, this gesture would be considered by some an excess of "woke-ism." But in the context of Carole King's question that had been bothering me, it struck me as a gesture of humble human connection. The story we were about to witness was taking place on land that was once the home of others. We (the audience, the actors, the original inhabitants) connected to one another at this place.

The place I now call home, with its alluring vistas and piney odor, served as home to many before me, and will serve as home to many after me. I am a passerby, hoping to catch your eye for the briefest of human connection. And while I am privileged to be able to move freely to new places, the home I seek is no different from the home millions of displaced refugees and immigrants seek—a place that offers human connection.

∽

Jan, I, and our kids found human connections, of course, in each of our many moves. Home, then, traveled from one place to another, now here and then there, and it found a place among the interstices of our wandering.

A selfie of Jan and me in front of our house on the day
we arrived in Tacoma. July 9, 2023.

Epilogue

I returned to [the Galapagos] islands...and my memory of them had altered, the way memories do, like parti-colored pebbles rolled back and forth over a grating, so that after a time those hard bright ones, the ones you thought you would never lose, have vanished, passed through the grating, and only a few big, unexpected ones remain, no longer unnoticed but now selected out for some meaning, large and unknown.

–Annie Dillard, "Teaching a Stone to Talk"

What does it mean to tell the story of one's life?

In his *Confessions*, Augustine of Hippo tells his story so that it aligns with the story of salvation, fall, and redemption. Along the way, he reflects on time, memory, and narrative.

While contemporary writers may not be explicitly interested in the story of salvation, they often tell their stories with such beauty that their lives become art. I think of Eudora Welty's *One Writer's Beginnings* or Richard Wright's *Black Boy* or Norman Maclean's *A River Runs Through It*. Their stories trouble with memory, time, and narrative, as Saint Augustine's *Confessions* did long ago and many others after him, including me, try to do now. If Augustine told his story to clarify his relationship with God, writers today seek, if not God, a pattern, a meaning, for their life. In doing so, hints about living a life—a type of redemption—emerge for both writer and reader.

Søren Kierkegaard, the great Danish philosopher, made the audacious claim that "the individual is the universal" and so his work confronts the angst, responsibility, and necessity of diving deeply into one's story so as to open a common humanity.

Recollections on a Road Between

A story is not *the truth*, but a road toward it.

In these passages, I have drifted between and among narratives of family, nation, career, religion, and culture to catch glimpses of that most elusive and wounded of subjects—myself.

I have written from a place between, replete with heartache and imbalance, restlessness, joy, grief, love, death, false starts, new beginnings, nowhere and now, here, in search of a home, a place of connection. In his *Confessions*, St. Augustine says "Our hearts are restless until they rest in you, O Lord."

These passages of text explore my rootless and restless passing through time and history—an effort to re-member in narrative and thus hint at a place, a meaning, large and unknown, perhaps even eternal, amidst the shaking and longing on my road between.

www.ingramcontent.com/pod-product-compliance
Lightning Source LLC
Chambersburg PA
CBHW051055160426
43193CB00010B/1198